Sustainability and Optimality of Public Debt

Michael Carlberg • Arne Hansen

Sustainability and Optimality of Public Debt

Second Edition

Physica-Verlag
A Springer Company

Prof. Dr. Michael Carlberg
Dr. Arne Hansen

Department of Economics
Helmut Schmidt University
Hamburg, Germany

Originally published under: Carlberg, M. within the series: Contributions to Economics

ISBN 978-3-642-32966-1 ISBN 978-3-642-32967-8 (eBook)
DOI 10.1007/978-3-642-32967-8
Springer Heidelberg New York Dordrecht London

Library of Congress Control Number: 2012954557

Printed on acid-free paper

Physica is a brand of Springer
Springer is part of Springer Science+Business Media (www.springer.com)

Preface

Public debt seems to be one of the most important and controversial issues of our time. In many countries, large and persistent budget deficits have continuously raised the ratio of public debt to GDP. After balanced budgets and even surpluses in the late 1990s, the United States has returned to deficits in recent years. As a result, the US debt ratio has been growing steadily. In the extreme case of Japan, public debt has grown to more than twice the size of GDP. Meanwhile, the German debt ratio has doubled since reunification. These developments raise serious concerns about debt sustainability. Consequently, there are increased political efforts to reduce future deficits. For instance, see the Maastricht Treaty, the Stability and Growth Pact and, more recently, the controversy over balanced-budget rules in Europe. Against this background, the present book provides a theoretical analysis regarding the sustainability and optimality of public debt.

Michael Carlberg
Arne Hansen

Contents in Brief

Contents

From what I have said, it must not be inferred that I consider the system of borrowing as the best calculated to defray the extraordinary expenses of the State. It is a system which tends to make us less thrifty - to blind us to our real situation.

David Ricardo (1817)

It would be difficult to convince a man possessed of 20,000 pounds, or any other sum, that a perpetual payment of 50 pounds per annum was equally burdensome with a single tax of 1000 pounds. He would have some vague notion that the 50 pounds per annum would be paid by posterity, and would not be paid by him; but if he leaves his fortune to his son, and leaves it charged with this perpetual tax, where is the difference whether he leaves him 20,000 pounds, with the tax, or 19,000 pounds without it? This argument of charging posterity with the interest of our debt, or of relieving them from a portion of such interest, is often used by otherwise well informed people, but we confess we see no weight in it.

David Ricardo (1820)

1 Introduction

The present monograph is concerned with the sustainability and optimality of public debt. The analysis will be conducted within the framework of neoclassical growth theory. Particularly it proves useful to consider the Solow model, the overlapping generations model and the infinite horizon model. Sustainability refers to the existence and the stability of the long-run equilibrium. Optimality relates to the path of public debt that maximizes discounted utility.

The government is in control of three instruments: the government purchase ratio, the budget deficit ratio and the tax rate. For the time being let the purchase ratio be given exogenously. Then the government can follow either of two strategies, it fixes the deficit ratio or the tax rate. If the government fixes the deficit ratio, then according to the government budget constraint the tax rate will be endogenous. On the other hand, if the government fixes the tax rate, the deficit ratio will become endogenous. Now it will be argued that a fixed deficit ratio can be sustained. A fixed tax rate, however, cannot be sustained. Under the second strategy, public debt per head will tend to explode, thereby squeezing private capital per head down to zero.

Optimality leads to the modified golden rule of public debt. In this sense, the optimal deficit ratio and the optimal tax rate will be derived. Should the government borrow from the private sector in order to restrain capital formation? Or should it lend money in order to stimulate capital formation?

The focus will be on the dynamics of public debt. To begin with, we shall establish the short-run equilibrium as well as the long-run equilibrium. Further, by means of phase diagrams, we shall look into the stability of the long-run equilibrium. Moreover we shall trace out the processes of adjustment induced by various macroeconomic shocks. The government raises the deficit ratio, it lowers the tax rate or increases the purchase ratio. The rate of labour growth rises, or the saving ratio goes up. How do public debt and private capital move over time? What does the chain of cause and effect look like? In addition we shall review different scenarios: the closed economy, the small open economy, and two countries. The small open economy adds the dynamics of the current account and of foreign debt. And in a two-country setting, fiscal policy in country 1 affects consumption in country 2.

These ideas are clearly reflected in the exposition. The monograph consists of three major parts, the closed economy (part I), the small open economy (part II), and two countries (part III). Each part in turn is composed of up to three chapters, the Solow model, the overlapping generations model, and the infinite horizon model. Within each chapter, there are up to four sections. In these sections, the government fixes either the deficit ratio or the tax rate. Alternatively the government fixes either the deficit per head or the tax per head.

For instance have a look at a fixed deficit ratio in a Solow model of a closed economy. At first, in section 3.1.1, we shall set out a simple model. Then, in sections 3.1.2 and 3.1.3, we shall introduce the short-run equilibrium and the long-run equilibrium. Some emphasis will be laid on the properties of the steady state. So far the deficit ratio was assumed to be given arbitrarily. Now, in section 3.1.4, we shall try to find out the optimal deficit ratio. Instead, in section 3.1.5, the optimal saving ratio will be determined. In section 3.1.6, we shall inquire into the stability of the long-run equilibrium, and in section 3.1.7 we shall keep track of the processes of adjustment. As an exception, in section 3.1.8, we shall discuss a budget surplus. To illustrate the results, in section 3.1.9, a numerical example will be presented. Coming to an end, section 3.1.10 provides a summary.

2 A Brief Survey of the Literature

A good deal of analysis has been performed on the sustainability and optimality of public debt. First of all regard a closed economy where the government fixes the deficit ratio (or, for that matter, the deficit per head). Diamond (1965) builds an overlapping generations model of a growing economy. The government makes public transfers. Specifically it fixes the deficit per head. Diamond postulates the existence and stability of a long-run equilibrium. He reaches the conclusion that budget deficits crowd out private investment. Phelps and Shell (1969) investigate a Solow model of a growing economy. Once again the government makes transfers and fixes the deficit per head. The authors demonstrate that there are two long-run equilibria, one of them being stable, the other unstable. Barro (1974) studies an overlapping generations model of a stationary economy, emphasizing the bequest motive. The government makes transfers and fixes the deficit per head. As a consequence, a steady state does indeed exist. He shows that, under these circumstances, budget deficits do not crowd out private investment (Ricardian equivalence). Carlberg (1984, 1985, 1988) starts from a Solow model of a growing economy, allowing for public consumption and public investment. The government fixes the deficit ratio. In this situation there is a unique long-run equilibrium. What is more, there exists an optimal deficit ratio. Further he probes into an overlapping generations model of a growing economy where the government makes transfers. The government fixes the deficit ratio. In this case there are two long-run equilibria. In addition the optimal deficit ratio is ascertained. Ihori (Optimal Deficits in a Growing Economy, 1988) constructs an infinite horizon model of a growing economy with public consumption as well as public investment. Assuming a constant saving ratio, he deduces the optimal deficit ratio. The monograph by Grill (1989), though written independently, is much in the same spirit as the paper by Ihori. Michaelis (1989) examines an overlapping generations model of a growing economy. The government either consumes or invests. It fixes the deficit ratio. Within this setting there are two steady states. And there exists an optimal deficit ratio. Beyond that he introduces the bequest motive and determines once more the optimal deficit ratio. Under these conditions, surprisingly, Ricardian equivalence does no longer hold.

At this point, we leave the fixed deficit ratio (the fixed deficit per head) and come to the fixed tax rate (the fixed tax per head, respectively). Carlberg (1983, 1988) considers a Solow model of a growing economy with public consumption and public investment. Particularly the government fixes the tax rate. He derives a necessary and sufficient condition for the existence of a long-run equilibrium. As a rule, there will be no long-run equilibrium whatsoever. As an exception, if the saving ratio is very high and if the primary deficit ratio is extremely low, there will be two long-run equilibria. To sum up, a fixed tax rate generally cannot be sustained. McCallum (1984) draws on an infinite horizon model of a stationary economy with public consumption. The government fixes the tax per head. As a result, a steady state does not exist. Schlieper (1984) takes the same approach as Carlberg. He concentrates on stability analysis by adopting phase-diagram techniques. The paper by Masson (1985) is based on an overlapping generations model of a growing economy with public consumption. The government fixes the tax per head. He implements a stability analysis by making use of phase diagrams. If the interest rate exceeds the natural rate, there will be no long-run equilibrium at all. On the other hand, if the interest rate falls short of the natural rate, there will be two long-run equilibria, a stable one and an unstable one. In the real world, of course, the interest rate is endogenous.

Tobin (1986) rests on an overlapping generations model of a growing economy with public consumption. The government fixes the tax rate. According to simulations, it may well happen that there is no (stable) steady state. Wenzel (1986) contemplates a Solow model of a growing economy with public consumption and public investment. Fiscal policy safeguards the golden rule. The government fixes the tax rate. In this instance there exists a unique long-run equilibrium. Over and above that a stability condition obtains. Ihori (Debt Burden and Intergeneration Equity, 1988) designs an overlapping generations model of a growing economy with public consumption. The government fixes the tax per head. He carries out a stability analysis by employing phase diagrams. Possibly there are two steady states, one of them being stable, the other unstable. Zee (1988) discusses an overlapping generations model of a growing economy with public consumption. The government fixes the tax rate. The necessary condition of stability is that the net interest rate stays below the natural rate. But the interest rate is endogenous. Michaelis (1989) looks into an overlapping generations model of a growing economy with public consumption. The government fixes the tax rate. He establishes a necessary and sufficient condition for the existence of a long-run equilibium. As a rule, there will be no steady state. As an exception, if the future consumption elasticity is very large and if the primary deficit ratio is extremely small, there will be two steady states. In this sense, a fixed tax rate is not feasible in the long run. Schmid (1990) evaluates an overlapping generations model of a growing economy with public consumption. The government fixes the tax per head. He conducts a stability analysis with the help of phase diagrams. Technology and preferences are of the Cobb-Douglas type, which seems to be an important special case. As a finding, there may exist two long-run equilibria, a stable one and an unstable one.

We turn next to the open economy. Carlberg (External versus Internal Public Debt 1985, Public Debt 1988) contains a Solow model of a growing economy with public consumption. The government fixes the deficit ratio. The model exhibits an unique steady state. In addition there is an optimal deficit ratio. Batina and Ihori (A Dynamic Analysis of the Optimal Provision, 1989) offer an overlapping generations model of a stationary economy with public consumption. They arrive at the optimal path of public debt over an infinite horizon. Carlberg (1993) reviews an overlapping generations model of a stationary economy with public consumption. The government fixes the tax rate. As a result, there exists no long-run equilibrium.

Finally a few words will be said on a world economy made up of two countries. Schmid (1988, 1990) features an overlapping generations model of a growing economy with public consumption. The government fixes the tax per head. He performs a stability analysis, applying phase diagrams. Production und utility functions are of the Cobb-Douglas variety. As an outcome, possibly there are two steady states, one of them being stable, the other unstable. Batina and Ihori (The Chain-Letter Debt Mechanism in a World Economy, 1989) explore an overlapping generations model of a stationary economy with public goods. The government fixes the tax per head. Stability analysis by means of phase diagrams reveals that the path can be either divergent or convergent. Carlberg (1993) relies on an overlapping generations model of a stationary economy with public consumption. The government fixes the tax rate. There is no long-run equilibrium, hence this strategy cannot be sustained.

Part I

The Closed Economy

3 The Solow Model

3.1 Fixing the Deficit Ratio

3.1.1 A Simple Model

To illustrate the basic idea, consider a simple model of public debt dynamics. The government borrows a certain fraction of national income $B = bY$. Here B denotes the budget deficit, Y is national income, and b is the deficit ratio. Strictly speaking, the government fixes the deficit ratio. The budget deficit in turn augments public debt $\dot{D} = B$, where D is public debt and the dot symbolizes the time derivative. This implies $\dot{D} = bY$. Now it is convenient to do the analysis in per capita terms. N stands for labour, $d = D/N$ is public debt per head and $y = Y/N$ is income per head. Next take the time derivative of public debt per head $\dot{d} = \dot{D}/N - D\dot{N}/N^2$, observing $\dot{D} = bY$. Moreover let labour grow at a constant rate $\dot{N} = nN$, with n being the natural rate. From this follows:

$$\dot{d} = by - nd \tag{1}$$

Here b, n and y are given exogenously. In the steady state, public debt per head does no longer move $\dot{d} = 0$, which yields:

$$d = by/n \tag{2}$$

Finally have a look at stability. Differentiate (1) for d to get $\partial\dot{d} / \partial d = -n < 0$. Therefore the steady state will be restored automatically. In the real world, however, income per head appears to be endogenous. An increase in the deficit ratio, for example, will reduce investment, capital and thus output.

3.1.2 The Short-Run Equilibrium

In sections 3.1.2 to 3.1.10, the simple model will be succeeded by a more sophisticated one. The investigation will be carried out within the following framework. Firms produce a single commodity Y by means of capital K and labour N. For ease of exposition, assume a Cobb-Douglas technology with constant returns to scale $Y = K^{\alpha}N^{\beta}$, $\alpha > 0$, $\beta > 0$ and $\alpha + \beta = 1$. Full employment does always prevail. Output Y can be devoted to consumption, investment and government purchases $Y = C + I + G$. Firms maximize profits $\Pi = Y - rK - wN$ under perfect competition. Here Π denotes profits, r the interest rate, and w the wage rate. As a consequence, the interest rate corresponds to the marginal product of capital $r = \partial Y/\partial K = \alpha Y/K$. In full analogy, the wage rate corresponds to the marginal product of labour $w = \partial Y/\partial N = \beta Y/N$.

We come now to the dynamics of public debt. The government raises loans and levies an income tax in order to finance government purchases and the interest payments on public debt. The government spends a fixed share of national income on goods and services $G = gY$ with purchase ratio g = const. Besides the government borrows a specified proportion of national income $B = bY$ with deficit ratio b = const. The budget deficit in turn adds to public debt $\dot{D} = B$. The government pays the interest rate r on public debt D, so public interest amounts to rD. The government imposes a tax at the flat rate t on both factor income and debt income $T = t(Y + rD)$. Accordingly, the government budget constraint can be written as $B + T = G + rD$. Taking account of the behavioural functions, the identity can be reformulated in the following way $bY + t(Y + rD) = gY + rD$. In this equation, the purchase ratio and the deficit ratio are given, whereas the tax rate must be adjusted appropriately.

We are concerned next with capital dynamics. Disposable income is the sum of debt income and factor income, net of taxes respectively $Y_d = Y + rD - T$. Households save a certain fraction of disposable income $S = sY_d$ with saving ratio s = const. A good deal of private savings is absorbed by public borrowing, the remainder being left for private investment $I = S - B$. On its part, private investment contributes to the accumulation of private capital $\dot{K} = I$. By backward substitution one obtains $\dot{K} = s(Y + rD - T) - B$. Further note $B + T = G + rD$, B

$= bY$ and $G = gY$ to reach $\dot{K} = (1 + b - g)sY - bY$. Last but not least, let labour expand at the natural rate $\dot{N} = nN$ with n = const.

Taking all pieces together, the short–run equilibrium can be represented by a system of six equations:

$$Y = K^{\alpha} N^{\beta} \tag{1}$$

$$r = \alpha Y / K \tag{2}$$

$$\dot{K} = (1 + b - g)sY - bY \tag{3}$$

$$\dot{D} = bY \tag{4}$$

$$bY + t(Y + rD) = gY + rD \tag{5}$$

$$\dot{N} = nN \tag{6}$$

Here α, β, b, g, n, s, D, K and N are exogenous, while r, t, $\dot{D}$, $\dot{K}$, $\dot{N}$ and Y are endogenous.

Again it proves useful to implement the analysis in per capita terms. The production function can be restated as $y = k^{\alpha}$, where k = K/N symbolizes capital per head and y = Y/N output per head. Further take the time derivative of capital per head $\dot{k} = \dot{K} / N - K\dot{N} / N^2$ and pay attention to (3) to achieve $\dot{k} = (1 + b - g)sy - by - nk$. Similarly take the time derivative of public debt per head $\dot{d} = \dot{D} / N - D\dot{N} / N^2$. Then insert (4) to conclude $\dot{d} = by - nd$. In summary, the short-run equilibrium can be encapsulated in a system of five equations:

$$y = k^{\alpha} \tag{7}$$

$$r = \alpha y / k \tag{8}$$

$$\dot{k} = (1 + b - g)sy - by - nk \tag{9}$$

$$\dot{d} = by - nd \tag{10}$$

$$by + t(y + rd) = gy + rd \tag{11}$$

Here $\dot{d}$, $\dot{k}$, r, t and y adapt themselves suitably.

3.1.3 The Long-Run Equilibrium

In the long-run equilibrium, the movement of public debt per head and of capital per head comes to a halt $\dot{d} = 0$ and $\dot{k} = 0$. Hence the long-run equilibrium can be characterized by a system of five equations:

$$y = k^{\alpha} \tag{1}$$

$$r = \alpha y / k \tag{2}$$

$$nk = (1 + b - g)sy - by \tag{3}$$

$$nd = by \tag{4}$$

$$by + t(y + rd) = gy + rd \tag{5}$$

Here d, k, r, t and y accommodate themselves.

For the remainder of this section, the steady state values of the endogenous variables will be stated explicitly. Let us begin with capital per head. Eliminate y in (3) with the help of (1) and rearrange:

$$k^{\beta} = \frac{(1 + b - g)s - b}{n} \tag{6}$$

Next we shall determine the capital-output ratio $v = k/y$. By virtue of $v = k^{\beta}$, the capital-output ratio is the same size:

$$v = \frac{(1 + b - g)s - b}{n} \tag{7}$$

A rise in the deficit ratio generates a fall in the capital-output ratio. The same holds for an increase in the purchase ratio and the rate of labour growth, respectively. Yet a lift in the saving ratio pushes up the capital-output ratio. Why is the capital-output ratio inversely related to the deficit ratio? The reason is that the budget deficit crowds out investment, thereby reducing capital formation.

What is more, the analysis of (7) gives rise to a critical deficit ratio:

$$b' = \frac{(1-g)s}{1-s} \tag{8}$$

If $b \lesseqgtr b'$, then $v \gtreqless 0$. That means, under a low deficit ratio a long-run equilibrium does in fact exist. Under a high deficit ratio, on the other hand, there will be no long-run equilibrium whatsoever. Exactly for $b = b'$ fatal crowding out occurs $v = 0$. Owing to that b' may be called the fatal deficit ratio. In a numerical example with $g = 0.2$ and $s = 0.1$, the critical deficit ratio is $b' = 0.09$. In other words, public borrowing had better not to go beyond nine percent of national income.

Besides solve (4) for the debt-income ratio:

$$D/Y = b/n \tag{9}$$

Table 3.1 shows the debt-income ratio as a function of the deficit ratio, supposing $n = 0.03$. For instance, a deficit ratio of three percent involves a debt-income ratio of one hundred precent. Further get rid of v in $r = \alpha/v$ by recurring to (7):

$$r = \frac{\alpha n}{(1+b-g)s-b} \tag{10}$$

Due to (10), a boost in the deficit ratio drives up the interest rate. The underlying mechanism is that the budget deficit hinders capital accumulation, thus raising the marginal product of capital. Moreover combine (9) $d/y = b/n$ and (10) to end up with the share of public interest in national income:

$$\frac{rd}{y} = \frac{\alpha b}{(1+b-g)s-b} \tag{11}$$

Having laid this groundwork, we can try to find out the tax rate. Solve (5) for t, divide through by y and pay heed to (11):

$$t = \frac{\left[(1+b-g)s-b\right](g-b)+\alpha b}{(1+b-g)s-\beta b} \tag{12}$$

Table 3.1
Deficit Ratio and Debt-Income Ratio

b	D/Y
0	0
0.01	0.33
0.02	0.67
0.03	1.00
0.04	1.33

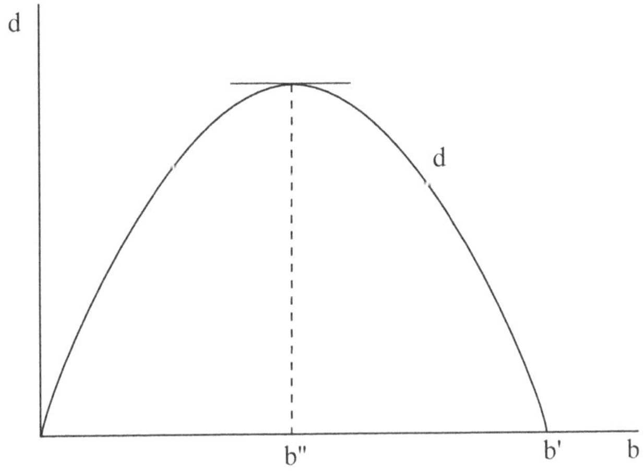

Figure 3.1
Deficit Ratio and Public Debt Per Head (Solow Model)

Finally a few comments are in place concerning public debt per head. Substitute (1) together with (6) into (4) and regroup terms:

$$d = \frac{b}{n}\left[\frac{(1+b-g)s-b}{n}\right]^{\alpha/\beta} \tag{13}$$

The effect of variations in the deficit ratio on public debt per head is ambiguous, see below. An increase in the purchase ratio (in the natural rate, respectively) causes a decline in public debt per head. But a rise in the saving ratio is accompanied by a rise in public debt per head. What is the intuition behind these results? As a point of departure take $d = by/n$. A lift in the deficit ratio cuts back income per head, so two counteracting forces are at work. An elevation of the purchase ratio depresses income per head and hence public debt per head. In the same vein, a speeding up of labour growth diminishes income per head and public debt per head. And a kick to the saving ratio enhances income per head as well as public debt per head.

How, precisely, does a change in the deficit ratio impinge on public debt per head? The evaluation of (13) furnishes another critical deficit ratio:

$$b'' = \frac{(1-g)\beta s}{1-s} \tag{14}$$

As long as the deficit ratio falls short of the critical level, an increase in the deficit ratio expands public debt per head. But as soon as the deficit ratio exceeds the critical level, the increase in the deficit ratio contracts public debt per head. Figure 3.1 displays public debt per head as a function of the deficit ratio. Obviously b'' is smaller than b'. In the numerical example with $\beta = 0.8$, $g = 0.2$ and $s = 0.1$, the critical deficit ratio is $b'' = 0.07$.

3.1.4 The Optimal Deficit Ratio

In the preceding sections, the deficit ratio was assumed to be given arbitrarily. In the current section, instead, we shall search for the optimal deficit ratio. The natural criterion for efficiency is to maximize the sum of consumption and government purchases, in per capita terms respectively. Under the golden rule the interest rate harmonizes with the natural rate $r = n$. This together with $r = \alpha/v$ delivers $v = \alpha/n$. Compare this with (7) from section 3.1.3 to obtain the optimal deficit ratio:

$$b^* = \frac{(1-g)s-\alpha}{1-s} \tag{1}$$

In the numerical example with $\alpha = 0.2$, $g = 0.2$ and $s = 0.1$, the optimal deficit ratio is negative $b^* = -0.13$. In this instance the goverment should run a budget surplus, thereby piling up public assets. Generally there exists a critical saving ratio:

$$s' = \frac{\alpha}{1-g} \tag{2}$$

If $s \gtrless s'$ then $b^* \gtrless 0$. In the first case, capital is abundant. Against this background the government should raise loans in order to restrain capital formation. In the second case, capital is scarce. The other way round, the government should lend money to the private sector in order to stimulate capital formation. In the numerical example with $\alpha = 0.2$ and $g = 0.2$, the critical saving ratio seems to be rather great $s' = 0.25$. What about the optimal tax rate? On account of $r = n$, $nd = by$ can be expressed as $rd = by$. Put this into (5) from section 3.1.3 and reshuffle adequately: $t = g/(1 + b)$. Then note (1) to reach the optimal tax rate:

$$t^* = \frac{(1-s)g}{\beta - gs} \tag{3}$$

In the numerical example, the optimal tax rate $t^* = 0.23$ surpasses the purchase ratio.

An increase in the purchase ratio lowers the optimal deficit ratio and raises the optimal tax rate. How can this be explained? A rise in government purchases is associated with a rise in taxation, which deteriorates savings. In order to prevent undercapitalization, the government narrows the budget deficit. Conversely a jump in the saving ratio pushes up the optimal deficit ratio. In addition it pulls down the optimal tax rate, provided $\beta > g$. A rise in the saving ratio improves savings. In order to avoid overcapitalization, the government widens the budget deficit.

3.1.5 The Optimal Saving Ratio

So far we relied on the premise that the saving ratio is exogenous. Now, in place of that, we shall ascertain the optimal saving ratio. Put another way, which saving ratio maximizes the sum of consumption and government purchases, per head respectively. Under the golden rule it applies that $v = \alpha/n$. Equate this with (7) from section 3.1.3 and solve for the optimal saving ratio:

$$s^* = \frac{\alpha + b}{1 + b - g} \tag{1}$$

Of course the deficit ratio is fixed in this context. Table 3.2 exhibits the optimal saving ratio as a function of the deficit ratio. The numerical example rests on the specification $\alpha = 0.2$ and $g = 0.2$. Given a deficit ratio of three percent, the optimal saving ratio amounts to 28 percent. In the real world, however, the saving ratio seems to stay close to ten percent.

Table 3.2
Deficit Ratio and Optimal Saving Ratio

b	s*
0	0.25
0.01	0.26
0.02	0.27
0.03	0.28
0.04	0.29

3.1.6 Stability

In this section we shall look into the stability of the long-run equilibrium by adopting phase diagram techniques. Principally the short-run equilibrium can be compressed to a system of two differential equations:

$$\dot{d} = p(d,k) \tag{1}$$

$$\dot{k} = q(d,k) \tag{2}$$

First consider the $\dot{d} = 0$ demarcation line. Substitute $y = k^{\alpha}$ into $\dot{d} = by - nd$ to verify:

$$\dot{d} = bk^{\alpha} - nd \tag{3}$$

Then differentiate (3) for d to realize $\partial\dot{d}/\partial d = -n < 0$. Further set $\dot{d} = 0$ and rearrange:

$$k = (nd/b)^{1/\alpha} \tag{4}$$

Figure 3.2 portrays the upward sloping $\dot{d} = 0$ line for the case $b > 0$. Second regard the $\dot{k} = 0$ demarcation line. Eliminate y in $\dot{k} = (1 + b - g)sy - by - nk$ with the help of $y = k^{\alpha}$ to get:

$$\dot{k} = \left[(1 + b - g)s - b\right]k^{\alpha} - nk \tag{5}$$

Then differentiate (5) for k and evaluate the derivative at the long-run equilibrium with $k^{\beta} = [(1 + b - g)s - b]/n$ to attain $\partial\dot{k}/\partial k < 0$. Moreover set $\dot{k} = 0$ and solve for k:

$$k^{\beta} = \frac{(1 + b - g)s - b}{n} \tag{6}$$

Evidently (6) does not depend on d, so the $\dot{k} = 0$ line is horizontal, see figure 3.2. Assembling all component parts, figure 3.2 contains the phase diagram. Here the long-run equilibrium lies in the intersection of the demarcation lines. The long-run equilibrium is stable, as can be learnt from the directional arrows.

To summarize, a long-run equilibrium does indeed exist, as long as the deficit ratio stays below the critical level. Over and above that, the long-run equilibrium proves to be stable. As a result, a fixed deficit ratio generally can be sustained.

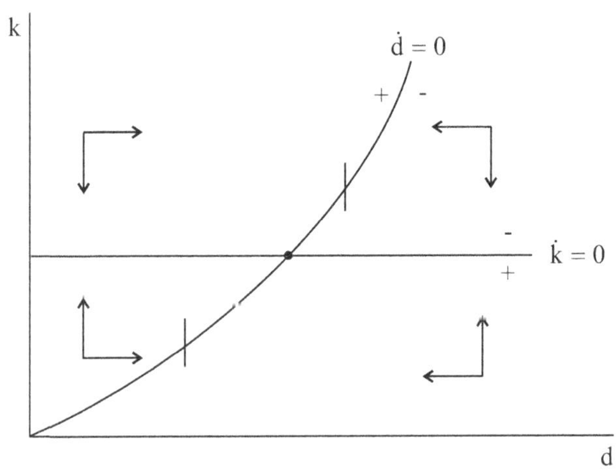

Figure 3.2
Fixed Deficit Ratio (Solow Model)

3.1.7 Some Shocks

In the current section we shall trace out in greater detail the processes of adjustment induced by five macroeconomic shocks:
- an increase in the deficit ratio ($b < b'$)
- an increase in the deficit ratio ($b > b'$)
- an increase in the purchase ratio
- an increase in labour growth
- an increase in the saving ratio.

Let us begin with a rise in the deficit ratio. First contemplate the case that the deficit ratio stays below the critical level. In this situation there exists a long-run equilibrium which proves to be stable. Initially the economy rests in the long-run equilibrium. The budget deficit and public debt, per capita respectively, do not move. Similarly investment and capital per head are uniform. Output and consumption per head do not change either. Against this background the government enhances the deficit ratio. In the phase diagram, therefore, both demarcation lines shift downwards, cf. figure 3.3. And the streamline indicates how the economy travels through time.

In the short run, output per head does not respond. The rise in the deficit ratio leads to a fall in investment per head. According to the budget constraint, the government is able to cut the tax rate, thereby lifting consumption per head. In the medium run, the increase in the deficit ratio augments public debt per head round by round. Conversely, the reduction in investment per head depresses capital per head period by period. The decline in capital per head goes along with a decline in output per head and consumption per head. The rise in both the interest rate and public debt per head contribute to a rise in public interest per head. To cover this, the government is bound to raise the tax rate.

As time proceeds, the economy converges to a new long-run equilibrium. The budget deficit and public debt, per capita respectively, do not move any longer. Likewise investment and capital per head are again invariant. Output as well as consumption per head come to a standstill. More exactly, the terminal

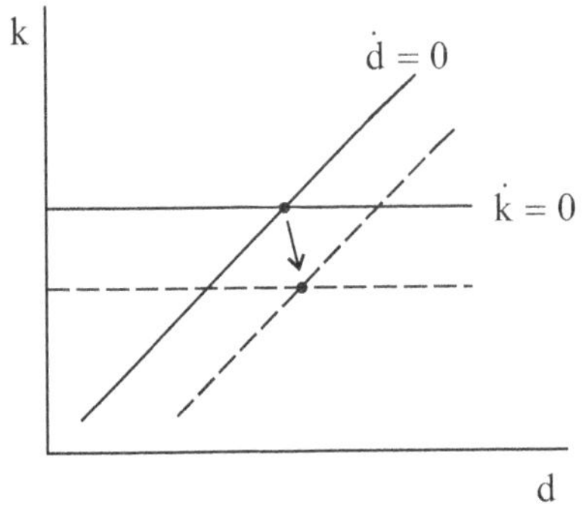

Figure 3.3
Increase in Deficit Ratio (b < b')

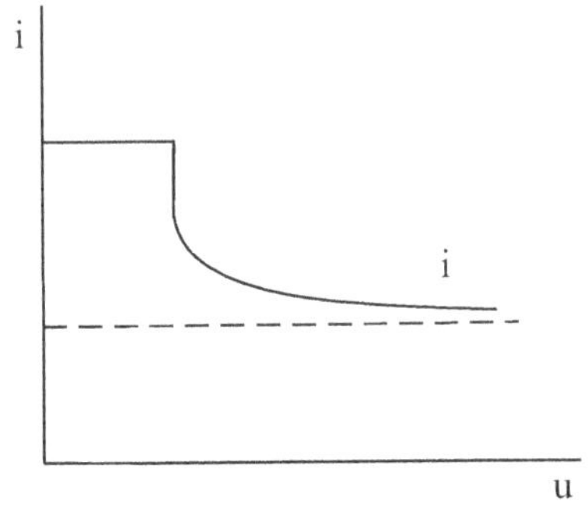

Figure 3.4
Investment Per Head

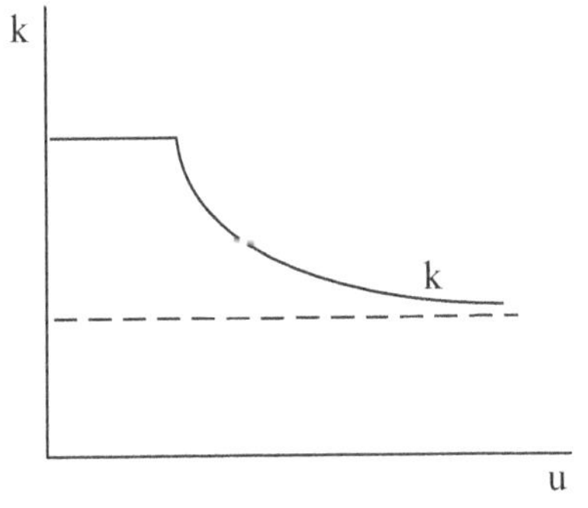

Figure 3.5
Capital Per Head

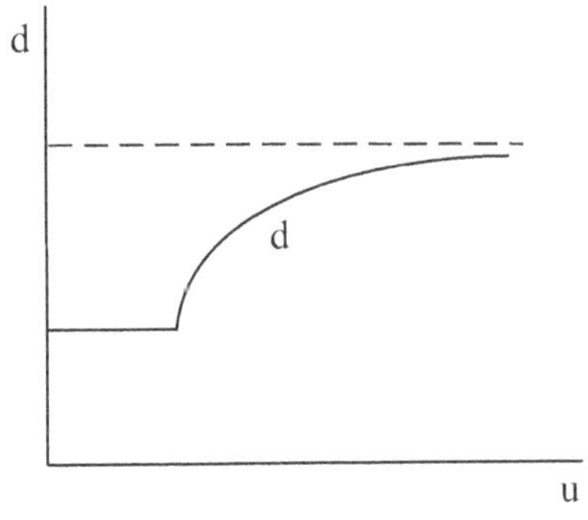

Figure 3.6
Public Debt Per Head

value of capital per head falls short of its initial value. The same is true of income per head and investment per head. Public debt per head ends up at a higher level, provided $b < b''$. The tax rate exceeds its original value, given $b > b'''$ (cf. section 3.1.9). And consumption per head will be smaller than before, as long as $b > b^*$. Figures 3.4 to 3.8 illuminate the time paths of the key variables.

Second we treat the case that the deficit ratio surpasses the critical level. Under these circumstances there will be no long-run equilibrium. At the start, let the economy reproduce itself in a steady state with $b < b'$. Public debt per head and capital per head are constant. Then suddenly the government lifts the deficit ratio above the critical level. In the short run, as a reaction, investment per head comes down. In the intermediate run, public debt per head grows step by step. That is why capital per head becomes dismantled piecemeal. The fall in capital per head entails a fall in output and income per head. This in turn diminishes savings and investment per head, thus accelerating the decline of capital per head. In this way the economy enters a vicious circle. In the long run, this process drives capital per head down to zero. In other words there will be fatal crowding out. Ultimately the economy must break down. Figures 3.9 and 3.10 throw some light on the pertinent trajectories. The equation of motion of public debt per head is $\dot{d} = by - nd$.

Third we address a hike in the purchase ratio, granted $b < b'$. In this situation there exists a long-run equilibrium that turns out to be stable. At the beginning, the economy is in the steady state. Public debt per head and capital per head do not stir. Then surprisingly the government pushes up the purchase ratio. In the phase diagram, the $\dot{k} = 0$ line shifts downwards, see figure 3.11. In the short run, on account of the budget constraint, the government has to raise the tax rate. But this lowers savings and investment per head. In the medium run, owing to the reduction in investment per head, capital per head decumulates. The contraction in capital and output per head brings about a contraction in the budget deficit per head. As a consequence, public debt per head shrinks gradually. In due course, the economy approaches a new steady state. Public debt per head and capital per head have adjusted completely. More precisely, both of these variables are smaller than before.

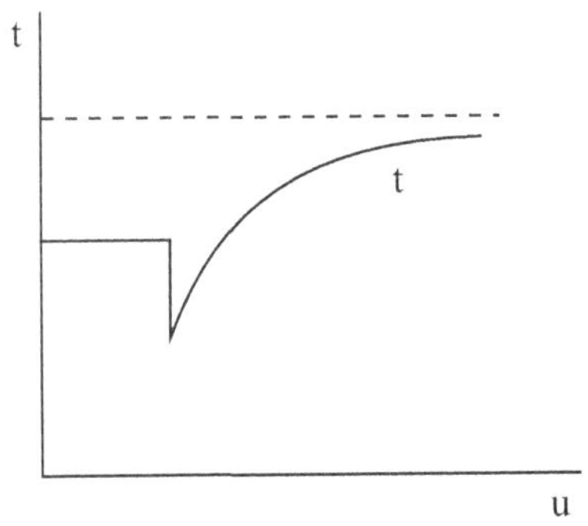

Figure 3.7
Tax Rate

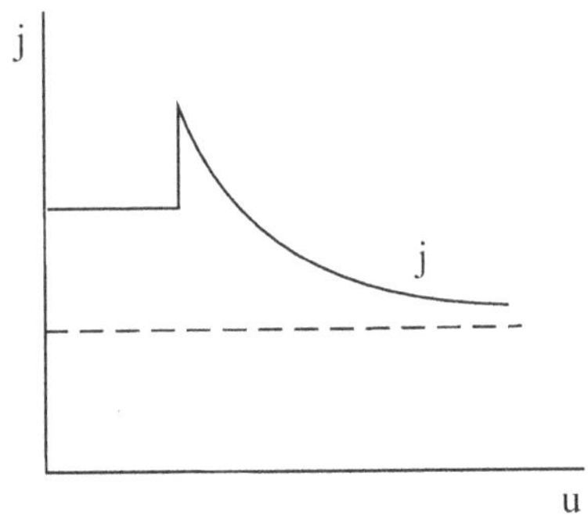

Figure 3.8
Consumption Per Head

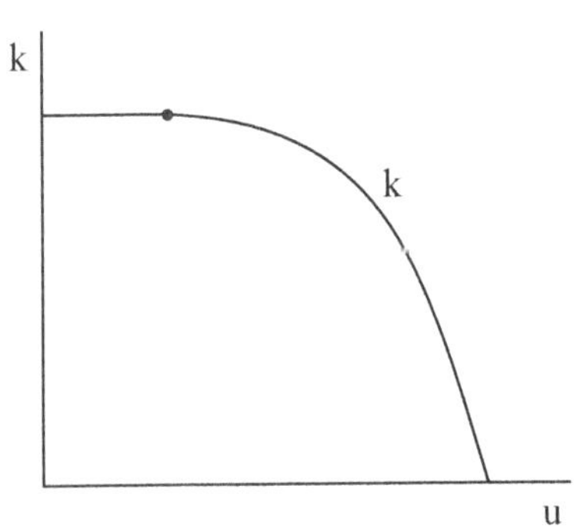

Figure 3.9
Capital Per Head (b > b')

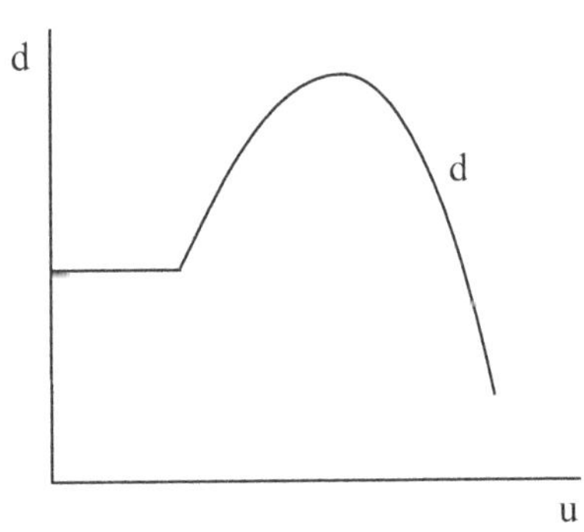

Figure 3.10
Public Debt Per Head (b > b')

Fourth we discuss a speeding up of labour growth. Originally the economy is in the stationary equilibrium. This idyllic condition is disrupted by a rise in the natural rate. In the phase diagram, the $\dot{d} = 0$ line jumps upwards, whereas the $\dot{k} = 0$ line plunges downwards, compare figure 3.12. In the short run, as measured by the growth rates, labour expands faster than output, so income per head drops. Therefore savings and investment per head are pulled down. For the same reason, the budget deficit per head is curtailed. In the intermediate run, capital per head becomes depleted. By the same token, public debt per head withers away. In the long run, public debt per head and capital per head settle down at a lower level.

Fifth we study a savings shock. At the start the economy rests in the long run equilibrium. Then abruptly the saving ratio springs up. In the phase diagram, the $\dot{k} = 0$ line is transposed upwards, cf. figure 3.13. In the short run, this elevates investment per head. In the medium run, capital per head begins to accumulate. Output, income and the budget deficit mount, in per capita terms respectively, thus heaping up public debt per head. Asymptotically the economy tends to a new long-run equilibrium. The post-shock values of both public debt per head and capital per head lie well above their pre-shock values.

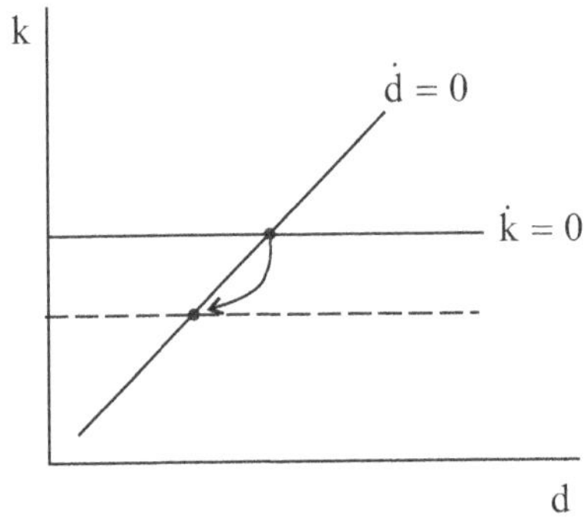

Figure 3.11
Increase in Purchase Ratio

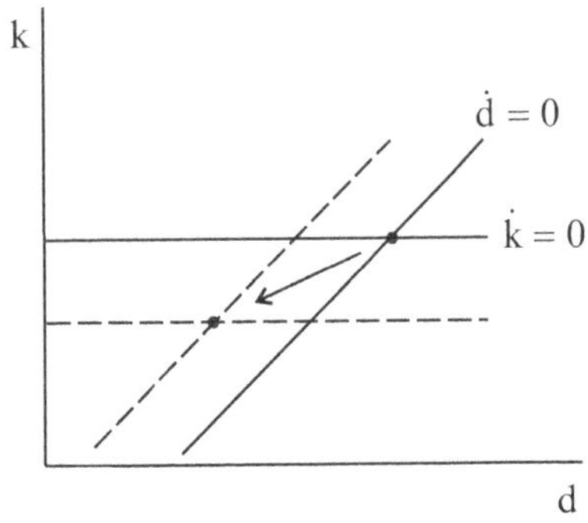

Figure 3.12
Increase in Labour Growth

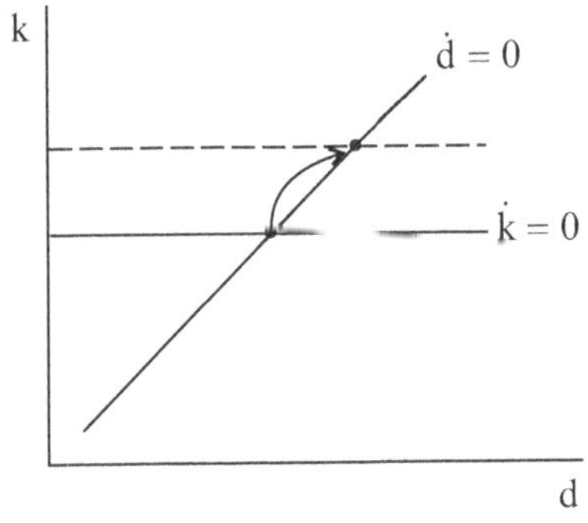

Figure 3.13
Increase in Saving Ratio

3.1.8 A Budget Surplus

As a rule, in the preceding sections, we assumed that the government runs a budget deficit. As an exception, in the current section, we postulate a budget surplus. Here the accent will be put on dynamics. Z stands for the budget surplus, z is the surplus ratio, A is public assets (i. e. private bonds held by the government), and a is public assets per head.

The differential equation $\dot{d} = bk^{\alpha} - nd$, well known from section 3.1.6, can be reinterpreted as:

$$\dot{a} = zk^{\alpha} - na \tag{1}$$

Evidently it holds $\partial\dot{a} / \partial a = -n < 0$. Now set $\dot{a} = 0$ to deduce:

$$k = (na / z)^{1/\alpha} \tag{2}$$

Figure 3.14 graphs the positively inclined $\dot{a} = 0$ line. Analogously $\dot{k} = [(1 + b - g)s - b]k^{\alpha} - nk$ can be rewritten as:

$$\dot{k} = [(1 - g - z)s + z]k^{\alpha} - nk \tag{3}$$

This furnishes $\partial\dot{k} / \partial k < 0$. Then set $\dot{k} = 0$ and regroup:

$$k^{\beta} = \frac{(1 - g - z)s + z}{n} \tag{4}$$

Figure 3.14 plots the horizontal $\dot{k} = 0$ line. Putting all pieces together, figure 3.14 offers the phase diagram. Apparently a long-run equilibrium does always exist. What is more, it proves to be stable. Thus, a fixed surplus ratio can be sustained.

Next have a look at the process of adjustment precipitated by an increase in the surplus ratio. Initially the economy reproduces itself in the steady state. The budget surplus and public assets, in per capita terms respectively, do not move. Investment and capital per head are uniform. Against this background, the gov-

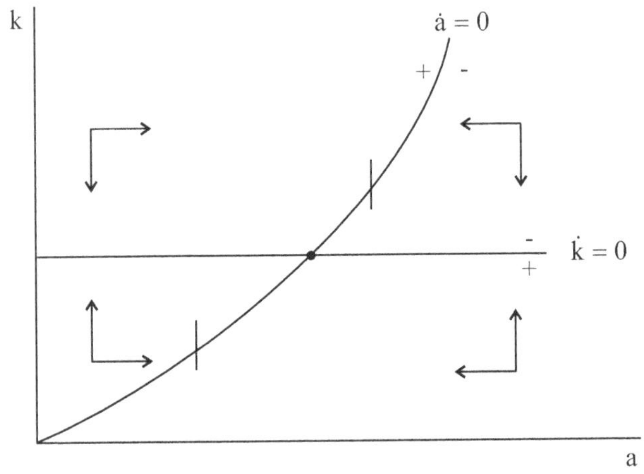

Figure 3.14
Fixed Surplus Ratio (Solow Model)

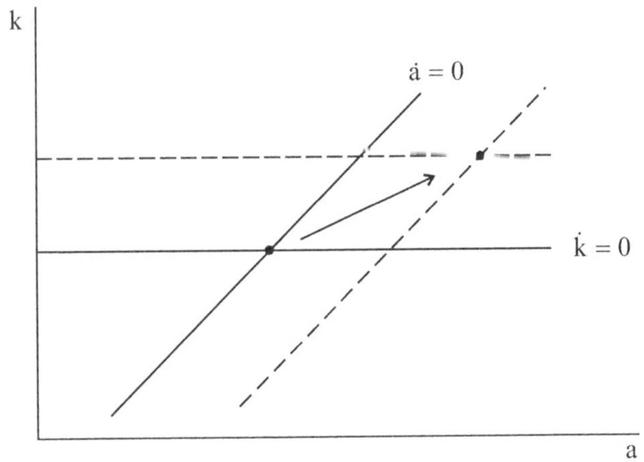

Figure 3.15
Increase in Surplus Ratio

ernment enhances the surplus ratio. In the phase diagram, the $\dot{a} = 0$ line comes down, while the $\dot{k} = 0$ line goes up, compare figure 3.15. In the short run, the increase in the surplus ratio brings up investment per head. According to the budget constraint, the government must raise the tax rate, thereby impeding consumption per head. In the intermediate run, the hike of the surplus ratio causes a piling up of public assets per head. Similarly the addition to investment per head contributes to capital formation per head. In due course the economy approaches a new steady state. Public assets and capital, in per capita terms, cease to move. During transition they have climbed to a higher level.

3.1.9 A Numerical Example

To illustrate this, take a numerical example. Table 3.3 gives the long-run consequences of a budget deficit, the parameter values being $\alpha = 0.2$, $g = 0.2$, $n = 0.03$ and $s = 0.1$. An increase in the deficit ratio b lowers the capital-output ratio v as well as the aggregate of consumption and government purchases per head j. Conversely it raises the interest rate r and the tax rate t. What happens when the deficit ratio comes close to the critical value of 0.09? The capital-output ratio as well as consumption and government purchases per head tend to zero, the tax rate tends to unity, and the interest rate tends to infinity.

By way of contrast, table 3.4 presents the long-run implications of a budget surplus. A rise in the surplus ratio z is associated with a rise in the capital-output ratio and a fall in the interest rate. As far as the tax rate (consumption and government purchases per head, respectively) is concerned, everything depends on the level of the surplus ratio. A rise in the surplus ratio at first reduces the tax rate. At a surplus ratio of $z = 0.04$, the tax rate attains a minimum of $t = 0.18$, being less than the purchase ratio $g = 0.20$. Then a further rise of the surplus ratio enhances the tax rate. Consumption and government purchases per head at first expand and later on contract, as the surplus ratio glides upwards. At a surplus ratio of 0.13, the goal function reaches a maximum of 1.29.

At this junction the diverse concepts of a critical deficit ratio will be compared briefly. First, the optimal deficit ratio is $b^* = -0.13$. Second, the fatal deficit ratio is $b' = 0.09$. As soon as the actual deficit ratio surpasses this value, the capital-output ratio becomes negative, so the economy is bound to collapse. Third, a boost in the deficit ratio drives up public debt per head, on the premise that $b < b''$. The critical deficit ratio relevant here is $b'' = 0.07$. Fourth, for the critical deficit ratio $b''' = -0.04$, the tax rate arrives at a minimum. Last but not least, figures 3.16 to 3.19 illuminate how an increase in the deficit ratio affects the capital-output ratio, the interest rate, the tax rate as well as the aggregate of consumption and government purchases per head.

Table 3.3
The Long-Run Effects of a Budget Deficit

b	v	r	t	j
0	2.7	0.08	0.20	1.18
0.01	2.4	0.09	0.21	1.15
0.02	2.1	0.10	0.23	1.13
0.03	1.8	0.11	0.25	1.09
0.04	1.5	0.14	0.29	1.05
0.05	1.2	0.17	0.34	1.00
0.06	0.9	0.23	0.41	0.94
0.07	0.6	0.35	0.52	0.85
0.08	0.3	0.75	0.71	0.71
0.09	0	∞	1	0

Table 3.4
The Long-Run Effects of a Budget Surplus

z	v	r	t	j
0	2.7	0.08	0.20	1.18
0.01	3.0	0.07	0.19	1.20
0.02	3.3	0.06	0.19	1.21
0.03	3.6	0.06	0.18	1.23
0.04	3.9	0.05	0.18	1.24
0.05	4.2	0.05	0.19	1.25
0.06	4.5	0.05	0.19	1.26
0.07	4.8	0.04	0.19	1.27
0.08	5.1	0.04	0.20	1.27
0.09	5.4	0.04	0.20	1.28
0.10	5.7	0.04	0.21	1.28
0.11	6.0	0.03	0.21	1.28
0.12	6.3	0.03	0.22	1.29
0.13	6.6	0.03	0.23	1.29
0.14	6.9	0.03	0.24	1.29
0.15	7.2	0.03	0.25	1.28

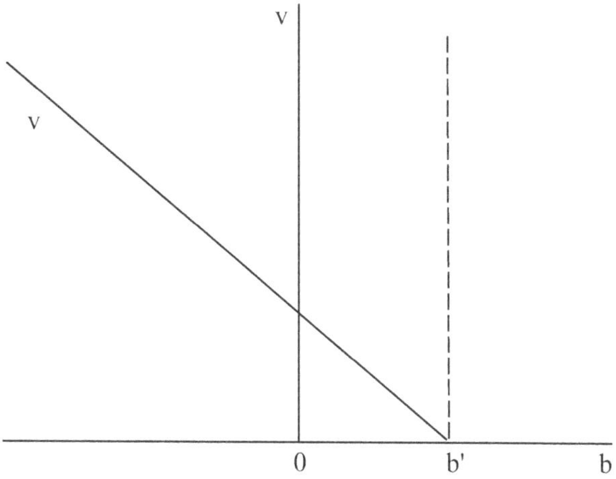

Figure 3.16
Deficit Ratio and Capital-Output Ratio

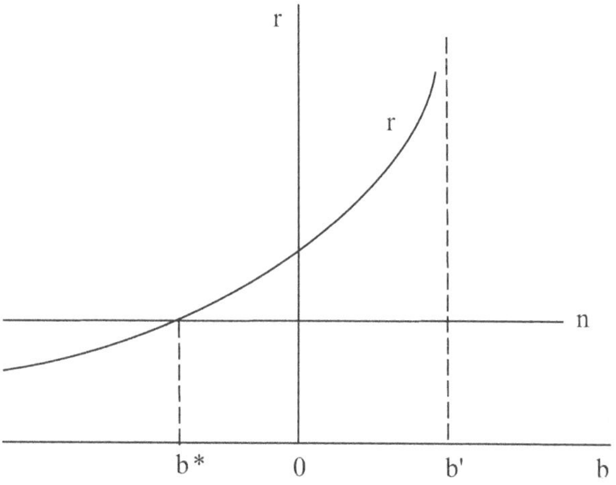

Figure 3.17
Deficit Ratio and Interest Rate

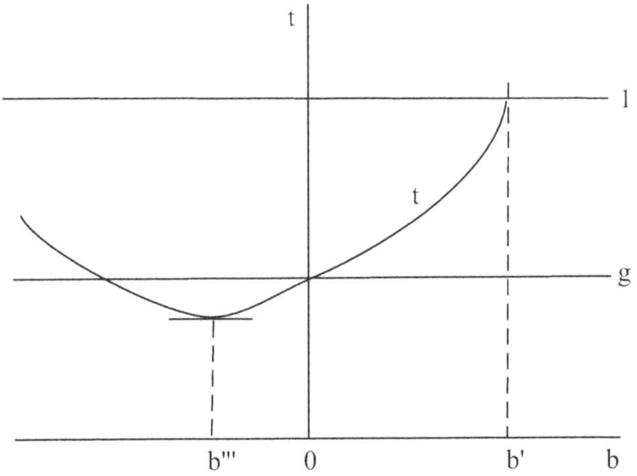

Figure 3.18
Deficit Ratio and Tax Rate

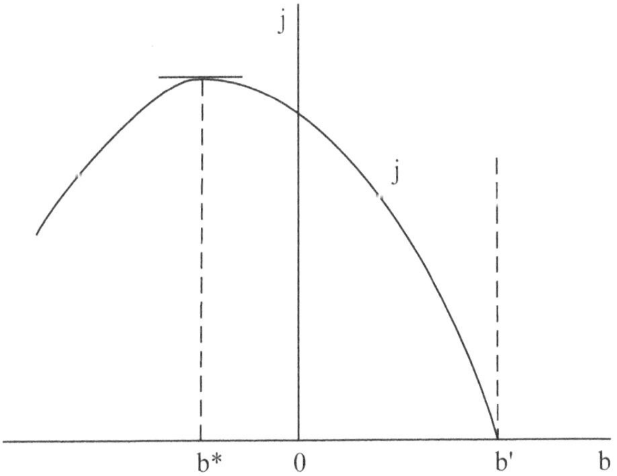

Figure 3.19
Deficit Ratio and "Consumption" per Head

3.1.10 Summary

An increase in the deficit ratio reduces both investment per head and capital per head. This leads to a critical deficit ratio. If the deficit ratio falls short of the critical value, there will be a long-run equilibrium that proves to be stable. But if the deficit ratio exceeds the critical value, there will be no long-run equilibrium at all. That is to say, under a low deficit ratio, a rise in the deficit ratio generates a fall in capital per head. Under a high deficit ratio, however, a further rise in the deficit ratio squeezes capital per head down to zero.

On the other hand, there exists an optimal deficit ratio that maximizes the aggregate of consumption and government purchases per head. Given a large saving ratio, the optimal deficit ratio is positive. In this case, the government should raise loans in order to restrain capital formation. As opposed to that, given a small saving ratio, the optimal deficit ratio is negative. In this case, the government should lend money to the private sector in order to stimulate capital formation. Casual evidence suggests that the government should extend credit. To summarize, a fixed deficit ratio generally can be sustained.

3.2 Fixing the Tax Rate

3.2.1 A Simple Model

In section 3.1, we started from the premise that the government fixes the deficit ratio. Instead, in section 3.2, we shall suppose that the government fixes the tax rate. To get a feeling of the basic idea, regard a simple model of budget dynamics. The government buys goods and services in a certain proportion to national income $G = gY$ with purchase ratio $g = \text{const}$. In addition the government collects a tax at a flat rate $t = \text{const}$ on both factor income and debt income $T = t(Y + rD)$. The budget deficit is defined as the excess of government purchases and public interest over tax revenue $B = G + rD - T$. The budget deficit in turn augments public debt $\dot{D} = B$. From this follows $\dot{D} = gY + rD - t(Y + rD)$. Now it is helpful to perform the analysis in per capita terms. Take the time derivative of public debt per head $\dot{d} = \dot{D}/N - D\dot{N}/N^2$ and observe $\dot{D} = gY + rD - t(Y + rD)$. Moreover let labour grow at the natural rate $\dot{N} = nN$ with $n = \text{const}$. This yields:

$$\dot{d} = gy + rd - t(y + rd) - nd \tag{1}$$

Here g, n, r, t and y are exogenous. In the steady state, public debt per head stops to change $\dot{d} = 0$. Put this into (1) and regroup:

$$d = \frac{gy - ty}{n - (1 - t)r} \tag{2}$$

To simplify matters, the investigation will be restricted to the case $t < g$. Correspondingly the evaluation of (2) gives rise to two distinct subcases. If the net interest rate stays below the natural rate, then public debt per head will be positive. The other way round, if the net interest rate surpasses the natural rate, then public debt per head will be negative, which seems to be somewhat like a paradox. Finally check for stability. Differentiate (1) for d to accomplish $\partial\dot{d}/\partial d = (1 - t)r - n$. That means, as long as the net interest rate is less than the natural rate, the steady state will be stable. Yet as soon as the net interest rate is greater than the natural rate, the steady state will be unstable. In the real world, however, the interest rate will be endogenous, relying on the deeper parameters of the model. A tax cut, for instance, forces the government to borrow money. This displaces investment and capital, thus bidding up the interest rate.

3.2.2 The Short-Run Equilibrium

In sections 3.2.2 to 3.2.9, we shall build a more elaborate model. Consider again a Cobb-Douglas technology $Y = K^{\alpha}N^{\beta}$. The interest rate harmonizes with the marginal product of capital $r = \alpha Y/K$. And labour expands at the natural rate $\dot{N} = nN$. What about budget dynamics? The government spends a fixed fraction of national income on goods and services $G = gY$ with purchase ratio $g = \text{const}$. Further the government levies a proportionate tax on both factor income and debt income $T = t(Y + rD)$ with tax rate $t = \text{const}$. Government purchases plus public interest minus tax earnings constitute the budget deficit $B = G + rD - T$. The budget deficit in turn adds to public debt $\dot{D} = B$. From this one can infer $\dot{D} = gY + rD - t(Y + rD)$.

The next point refers to investment dynamics. Disposable income is made up of factor income and debt income, net after tax respectively, $Y_d = Y + rD - T$. Households save a given share of disposable income $S = sY_d$ with saving ratio $s = \text{const}$. That part of savings which is not claimed by public borrowing, will be used for investment $I = S - B$. Investment in turn contributes to the accumulation of capital $\dot{K} = I$. From this emerges $\dot{K} = s(Y + rD - T) - B$. Combine this with $T = t(Y + rD)$ and $\dot{D} = B$ to verify $\dot{D} + \dot{K} = s(1 - t)(Y + rD)$.

On this foundation, the short-run equilibrium can be captured by a system of five equations:

$$Y = K^{\alpha}N^{\beta} \tag{1}$$

$$r = \alpha Y / K \tag{2}$$

$$\dot{D} + \dot{K} = s(1 - t)(Y + rD) \tag{3}$$

$$\dot{D} = gY + rD - t(Y + rD) \tag{4}$$

$$\dot{N} = nN \tag{5}$$

Here α, β, g, n, s, t, D, K and N are exogenous, whereas r, $\dot{D}$, $\dot{K}$, $\dot{N}$ and Y are endogenous. This is in remarkable distinction to the strategy of fixing the deficit ratio, cf. section 3.1. There the deficit ratio was exogenous, while the tax rate was endogenous.

Besides it is convenient to reformulate the short-run equilibrium in per capita terms:

$$y = k^{\alpha} \tag{6}$$

$$r = \alpha y / k \tag{7}$$

$$\dot{d} + \dot{k} = s(1 - t)(y + rd) - nd - nk \tag{8}$$

$$\dot{d} = gy + rd - t(y + rd) - nd \tag{9}$$

Here $\dot{d}$, $\dot{k}$, r and y adjust themselves appropriately.

3.2.3 The Long-Run Equilibrium

In the steady state, the motion of public debt per head and of capital per head comes to a standstill $\dot{d} = \dot{k} = 0$. Accordingly the long-run equilibrium can be expressed by a system of four equations:

$$y = k^{\alpha} \tag{1}$$

$$r = \alpha y / k \tag{2}$$

$$nd + nk = s(1 - t)(y + rd) \tag{3}$$

$$nd = gy + rd - t(y + rd) \tag{4}$$

Here d, k, r and y adapt themselves.

In the current section, the limelight will be directed at the problem of whether a steady state does exist or not. To begin with, $r = \alpha y/k$ can be restated as $rd = \alpha dy/k = \alpha xy$, where $x = d/k$ is the debt-capital ratio. The debt-capital ratio proves to be a key variable. Over and above that, we inaugurate the primary deficit ratio $h = g - t$. On this basis, equations (3) and (4) can be written as:

$$nd + nk = (1 - t)sy + (1 - t)\alpha sxy \tag{5}$$

$$nd = hy + (1 - t)\alpha xy \tag{6}$$

Now divide equation (5) by equation (6) and reshuffle:

$$\frac{1 + x}{x} = \frac{(1 - t)(s + \alpha sx)}{h + (1 - t)\alpha x} \tag{7}$$

Then solve this quadratic equation for x:

$$x = -\frac{h + (\alpha - s)(1 - t)}{2\alpha(1 - s)(1 - t)} \pm \sqrt{\frac{[h + (\alpha - s)(1 - t)]^2}{[2\alpha(1 - s)(1 - t)]^2} - \frac{h}{\alpha(1 - s)(1 - t)}} \tag{8}$$

A steady state does exist if and only if the debt-capital ratio x is real and positive. To evaluate this condition take the reduced discriminant of (8) $U = [h + (\alpha - s)(1 - t)]^2 - 4\alpha h(1 - s)(1 - t)$. The discriminant vanishes at:

$$h_{1,2} = (1 - t)(\alpha + s - 2\alpha s) \mp (1 - t)\sqrt{4\alpha s(1 + \alpha s - \alpha - s)} \tag{9}$$

The closer inspection of (9) reveals that h_1 and h_2 are both real and positive with $h_1 < h_2$. x in turn is real and positive if and only if:

$$s > \alpha \text{ and } h \le h_1 \tag{10}$$

The proof can be found in the appendix to this section. That is to say, a long-run equilibrium does exist if and only if the saving ratio exceeds the capital elasticity and the primary deficit ratio stays below the critical level. As a fundamental result, this is the necessary and sufficient condition for a fixed tax rate to be feasible in the long run.

To illustrate the condition have a look at a numerical example with $\alpha = 0.2$ and $g = 0.2$. Table 3.5 shows the minimum tax rate that can be sustained t' as a function of the saving ratio. Under a saving ratio of 10 or 20 percent, the critical tax rate coincides with the purchase ratio $t' = g = 0.2$. Of course, as long as the actual tax rate corresponds to the purchase ratio, it can be sustained. But as soon as the actual tax rate falls short of the purchase ratio, it cannot be sustained any more. Under a saving ratio of 30 percent, the minimum sustainable tax rate is a little bit smaller than the purchase ratio $t' = 0.189 < g = 0.2$. If the actual tax rate surpasses the critical level of 18.9 percent, it will be feasible in the long run. If the actual tax rate is set below the critical level, however, it will not be feasible in the long run. Figure 3.20 visualizes how the minimum sustainable tax rate varies with the saving ratio.

Empirical evidence seems to suggest that a fixed tax rate cannot be sustained. On the other hand, there may be an exception to this rule. If both the saving ratio is very high and the primary deficit ratio is extremely low, then a fixed tax rate can indeed be sustained. In summary, a fixed tax rate is rather unlikely to be feasible in the long run.

Table 3.5
Minimum Sustainable Tax Rate

s	t'
0.1	0.2
0.2	0.2
0.3	0.189
0.4	0.160

Appendix

Evidently (8) can be put as $x = -P/Q \pm \sqrt{R}$. In addition, the reduced discriminant of (8) can be stated as $U = (h - h_1)(h - h_2)$. This gives rise to four cases. First, if $h_1 < h < h_2$, then $U < 0$. Second, if $h \leq h_1$ and $s \leq \alpha$, then $U \geq 0$ and $x < 0$. Proof: P is positive. Now square $\sqrt{R} < P/Q$ to confirm $x < 0$. Third, if $h \leq h_1$ and $s > \alpha$, then $U \geq 0$ and $x > 0$. In this case, P is negative. Next square $-P/Q > \sqrt{R}$ to check $x > 0$. Fourth, if $h \geq h_2$, then $U \geq 0$ and $x < 0$. Proof: Here P is positive. Finally square $\sqrt{R} < P/Q$ to see $x < 0$.

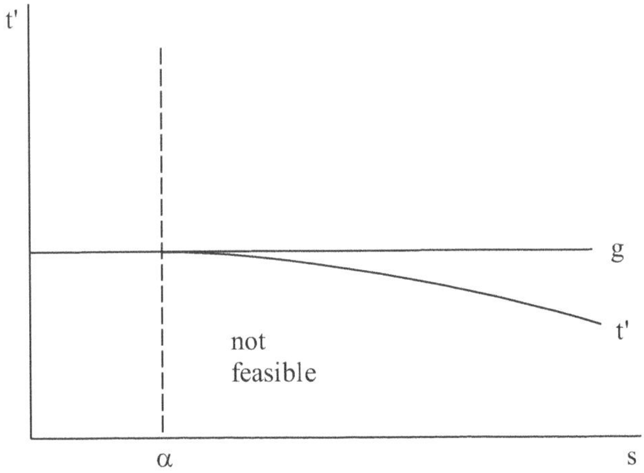

Figure 3.20
Saving Ratio and Minimum Sustainable Tax Rate

3.2.4 Stability

The short-run equilibrium can be to condensed to a system of two differential equations $\dot{d} = p(d, k)$ and $\dot{k} = q(d, k)$. At first we establish the $\dot{d} = 0$ demarcation line. Dispense with y in (9) by means of (6) from section 3.2.2, respectively:

$$\dot{d} = gk^{\alpha} + (1-t)rd - tk^{\alpha} - nd \tag{1}$$

Differentiate (1) for d to realize $\partial\dot{d}/\partial d = (1-t)r - n$. Here two situations can occur. If $(1-t)r \lesseqgtr n$, then $\partial\dot{d}/\partial d \lesseqgtr 0$. Now, in this condition, pay attention to $r = \alpha y / k = \alpha k^{-\beta}$, which involves a critical level of capital per head:

$$k' = [(1-t)\alpha / n]^{1/\beta} \tag{2}$$

Analogously, if $k \lesseqgtr k'$, then $\partial\dot{d}/\partial d \gtreqless 0$. Then set $\dot{d} = 0$ and solve (1) for d:

$$d = \frac{(g-t)k^{\alpha}}{n-(1-t)r} \tag{3}$$

This is the equation of the $\dot{d} = 0$ line. The interpretation of (3) will be restricted to the case $t < g$. By virtue of (3), if $(1-t)r \lesseqgtr n$, then $d \gtreqless 0$. In other words, as long as the net interest rate falls short of the natural rate, public debt per head will be positive. Yet as soon as the net interest rate exceeds the natural rate, public debt per head will become negative. This seems to be a contradiction in terms, so one may suspect that there will be no long-run equilibrium. Henceforth we postulate that the net interest rate stays below the natural rate, thus public debt per head will be positive. Further, as the net interest rate converges to the natural rate from below, public debt per head tends to explode. Similarly, in equation (3), take account of $r = \alpha k^{-\beta}$ and rearrange:

$$d = \frac{(g-t)k}{nk^{\beta} - (1-t)\alpha} \tag{4}$$

Owing to that, as k grows without limits, so does d. Having laid this groundwork, we can draw the $\dot{d} = 0$ line, cf. figure 3.21.

In the second step, we try to find out the $\dot{k} = 0$ demarcation line. Get rid of $\dot{d}$ in (8) by making use of (9) from section 3.2.2, respectively. Moreover note $y = k^{\alpha}$ and $r = \alpha y / k$ to ascertain:

$$\dot{k} = (s - st - g + t)k^{\alpha} - nk - (1 - s)(1 - t)\alpha d k^{-\beta} \tag{5}$$

As a corollary it holds $\partial \dot{k} / \partial d < 0$. Over and above that set $\dot{k} = 0$:

$$d = \frac{(s - st - g + t)k^{\alpha} - nk}{(1 - s)(1 - t)\alpha k^{-\beta}} \tag{6}$$

This is the equation of the $\dot{k} = 0$ line, which will be portrayed in figure 3.21, too. By the way, (6) vanishes at

$$k'' = [(s - st - g + t) / n]^{1/\beta} \tag{7}$$

The comparison of k' and k" yields a critical saving ratio:

$$s' = \frac{(1 - t)\alpha + g - t}{1 - t} \tag{8}$$

Due to that, if $s \lesseqgtr s'$, then $k' \gtreqless k''$. That means, under a small saving ratio, the demarcation lines do not cut, so a steady state does not exist. Conversely, under a large saving ratio, the demarcation lines can indeed intersect, so there may be a steady state. To explain this, consider a numerical example with $\alpha = 0.2$, $g = 0.2$ and $t = 0.19$. Under these circumstances, the critical saving ratio amounts to $s' = 0.21$. For the moment we assume that there is a steady state. The exact condition (necessary and sufficient) for the existence of a steady state was derived in section 3.2.3.

Assembling all component parts, figure 3.22 exhibits the complete phase diagram. Obviously there are two long-run equilibria k_1 and k_2 with $k_1 > k_2$. The high-level equilibrium k_1 turns out to be stable, whereas the low-level equilibrium k_2 is unstable.

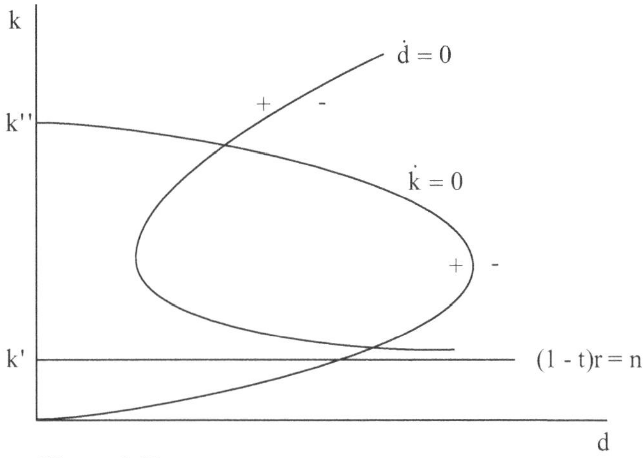

Figure 3.21
Fixed Tax Rate (Solow Model)

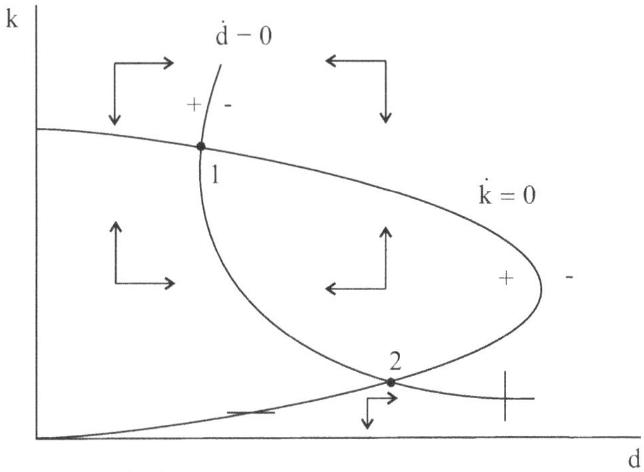

Figure 3.22
Fixed Tax Rate (Solow Model)

3.2.5 Some Shocks

Let the tax rate be smaller than the purchase ratio $t < g$. Then two situations can be distinguished. If $s \leq \alpha$ or $t < t'$, there will be no long-run equilibrium, cf. section 3.2.3. That is to say, if the saving ratio is low or if the tax rate falls short of the critical level, a fixed tax rate cannot be sustained. As opposed to that, if $s > \alpha$ and $t \geq t'$, there will in fact be a long-run equilibrium. Put another way, if the saving ratio is high and if the tax rate exceeds the critical level, a fixed tax rate can indeed be sustained. In the current section we shall keep track of the processes released by diverse government actions:

1) a permanent tax cut ($s \leq \alpha$, $t < g$)
2) a transitory tax cut ($s \leq \alpha$, $t < g$)
3) intertemporal budget balance ($s \leq \alpha$)
4) regime switching ($s \leq \alpha$)
5) a permanent tax cut ($s > \alpha$, $t \geq t'$)
6) a permanent tax cut ($s > \alpha$, $t < t'$)

1) Permanent tax cut ($s \leq \alpha$, $t < g$). In this case, a long-run equilibrium does not exist. At the beginning, without loss of generality, let the economy rest in a long-run equilibrium with $t = g$. The budget is balanced $b = 0$, so there is no public debt $d = 0$. Investment and capital per head, respectively, do not move. Output, income and consumption per head are uniform. Against this background, the government reduces the tax rate. In the short run, this disturbance has no effect on income per head. The tax cut enhances consumption per head. On the other hand, according to the budget constraint, the government must increase the deficit ratio, thereby depressing investment per head.

In the medium run, owing to the budget deficit, public debt starts to grow round by round, in per capita terms respectively. Likewise, due to the fall in investment per head, capital per head declines period by period. On account of the rise in public debt per head, the government has to make larger interest payments per head. Therefore the government must further increase the deficit ratio, which accelerates the growth of public debt per head. Beyond that, as debt income per head goes up, so does consumption per head.

In the long run, public debt per head tends to explode. This in turn drives capital per head down to zero. Obviously the economy enters a vicious circle where the government borrows in order to finance the interest payments on public debt. In other words, the tax cut leads to fatal crowding out. Eventually the economy must collapse. In this sense, the fixed tax rate is not feasible in the long run. Figures 3.23 to 3.25 depict the associated time paths of some main indicators.

2) Transitory tax cut ($s \leq \alpha$, $t < g$). In the specific case to be presented here the steady state proves to be unstable. Initially the economy reproduces itself in a steady state with $t = g$. The budget is again balanced $b = 0$, so there is no public debt $d = 0$. Then, all of a sudden, the government lowers the tax rate. This gives rise to a budget deficit, hence public debt begins to accumulate. To arrest the upward spiral, let the government raise the tax rate back to the original level. In spite of that, the budget remains in deficit, because of the interest payments the government has to make on the debt already incurred. As a consequence, with the lapse of time, public debt per head proliferates without bounds. That is why capital per head shrinks back to zero. Ultimately the economy must break down, even though the tax cut is only transitory in nature. Figure 3.26 visualizes the pertinent trajectories of some key variables.

3) Intertemporal budget balance ($s \leq \alpha$). At first the economy is once more in a stationary equilibrium with $t = g$. The budget is balanced $b = 0$, thus there is no public debt $d = 0$. Then surprisingly the government reduces the tax rate. The budget changes into deficit, hence public debt piles up. To counteract this, let the government increase the tax rate well above the purchase ratio. By virtue of that, the budget deficit turns into a surplus, thus redeeming public debt step by step. Strictly speaking, the tax rate has to be greater than the purchase ratio by a substantial amount, since public interest must also be covered. As soon as public debt has been brought down to zero again, the government can reduce the tax rate to the original level $t = g$. The budget is balanced again, so public debt will never reappear. In the long run, investment and capital per head settle down at their pre-shock levels. Figure 3.27 plots the required path of the tax rate, and figure 3.28 graphs how public debt per head and capital per head evolve over time.

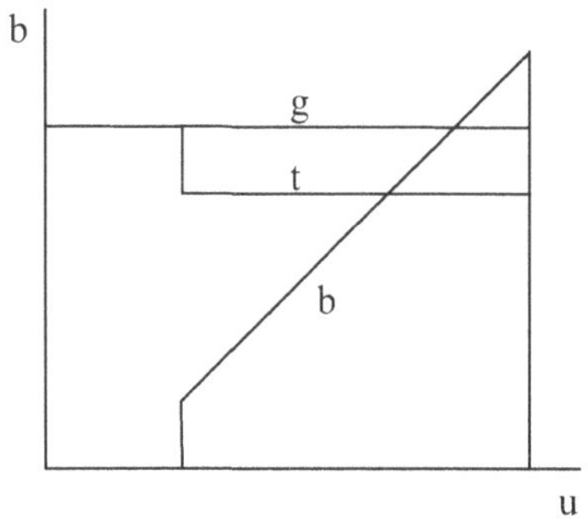

Figure 3.23
Permanent Tax Cut
$(s \leq \alpha,\ t < g)$

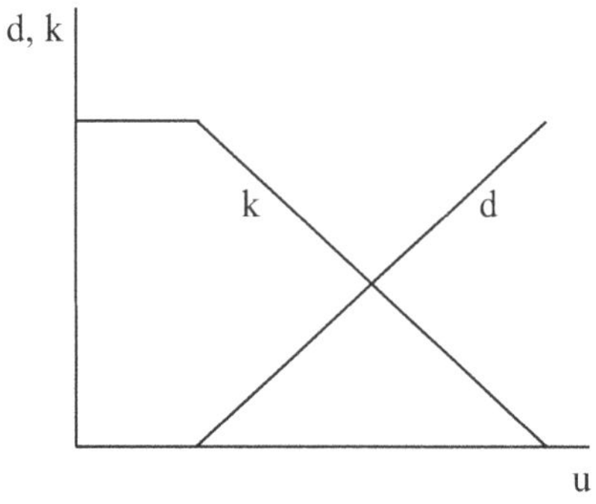

Figure 3.24
Permanent Tax Cut
$(s \leq \alpha,\ t < g)$

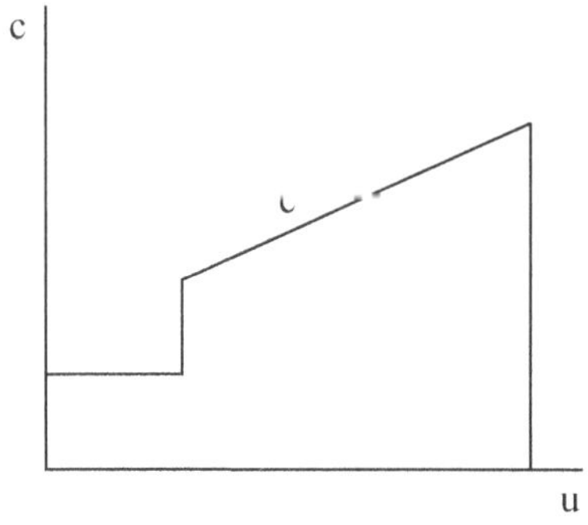

Figure 3.25
Permanent Tax Cut
$(s \leq \alpha,\ t < g)$

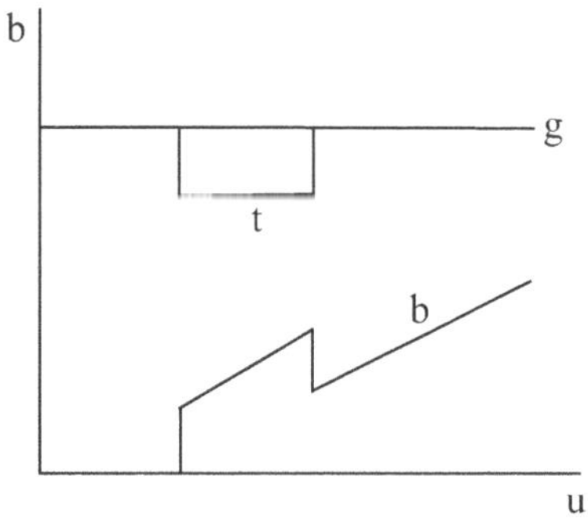

Figure 3.26
Transitory Tax Cut
$(s \leq \alpha,\ t < g)$

4) Regime switching ($s \leq \alpha$). At the start, the economy is in a long-run equilibrium with $t = g$. The budget balances, and no public debt does exist. Then, abruptly, the government cuts the tax rate. Correspondingly the government lifts the deficit ratio, hence public debt builds up gradually. Now, to put an end to this fatal process, let the government fix the deficit ratio at a low level. Therefore, due to the budget constraint, the government must push up the tax rate sharply, in such a way that it exceeds the purchase ratio by a distinct amount. This measure decreases public debt per head, so the government can pull down the tax rate slowly. In the long run, public debt per head ceases to move. Likewise, investment per head and capital per head converge to a lower level. Evidently the government switches the regime. It stops to fix the tax rate and, instead, begins to fix the deficit ratio. Under a fixed deficit ratio there exists a stable long-run equilibrium, as is familiar from section 3.1. Figure 3.29 shows the time paths of both the tax rate and the deficit ratio, before and after switch respectively. Figure 3.30 presents the stylized paths of public debt per head and capital per head.

5) Permanent tax cut ($s > \alpha$, $t \geq t'$). In this condition, there are two steady states, one of them being stable, the other unstable. Consider the stable case. Initially the economy reproduces itself in steady state number 1, cf. figure 3.31. The budget deficit and public debt, in per capita terms, do not vary. Investment per head and capital per head are constant. Similarly output, income and consumption per head do not stir. Against this background, the government lowers the tax rate. In the phase diagram, the $\dot{d} = 0$ line shifts to the right, whereas the $\dot{k} = 0$ line shifts to the left, cf. figure 3.31. The streamline indicates how the economy travels through time. In the short run, output per head remains unaffected. The drop in the tax rate elevates consumption per head. In addition, it enhances the deficit ratio, thereby displacing investment per head.

In the medium run, the increase in the deficit ratio gives rise to the accumulation of public debt per head. The other way round, the decline in investment per head calls forth the decumulation of capital per head. The other way round, the decline in investment per head calls forth the decumulation of capital per head. The fall in capital per head is accompanied by a fall in income per head and consumption per head. What is more, as the interest rate and public debt per head go up, so does public interest per head. And the reduction in income per head entails a reduction in tax proceeds per head. Both factors compel the government

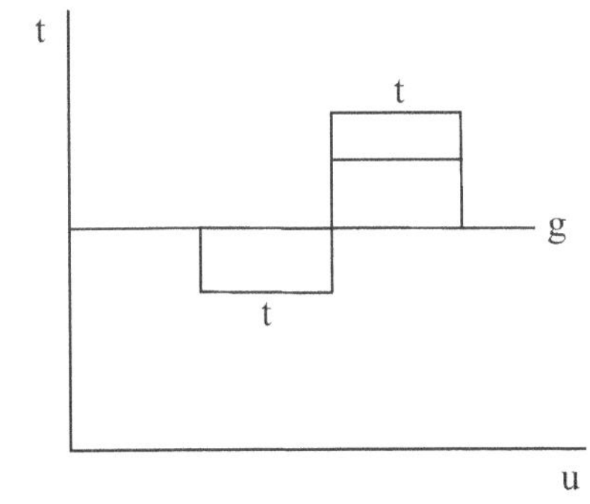

Figure 3.27
Intertemporal Budget Balance
(s ≤ α)

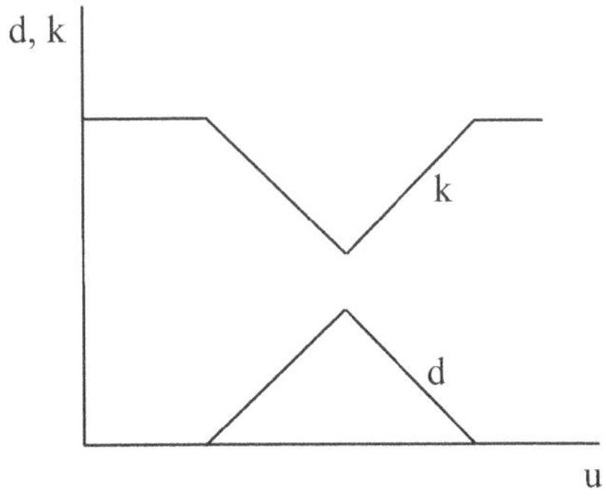

Figure 3.28
Intertemporal Budget Balance
(s ≤ α)

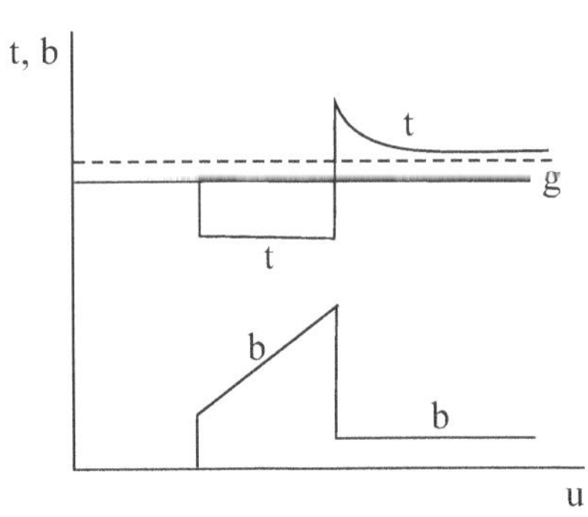

Figure 3.29
Regime Switching (s ≤ α)

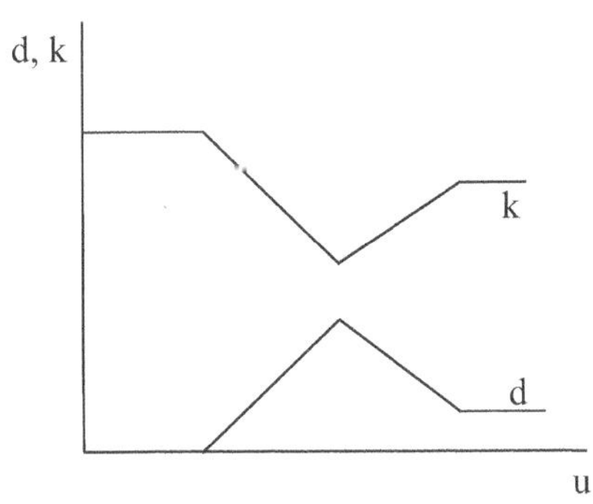

Figure 3.30
Regime Switching (s ≤ α)

to enhance the deficit ratio once again, thus further displacing investment per head. As a consequence, public debt per head continues to grow, while capital per head keeps on shrinking.

Asymptotically, the economy approaches a new steady state. The budget deficit and public debt, in per capita terms, do no longer vary. Investment per head and capital per head are again constant. Output and consumption per head come to a halt. Properly speaking, public debt per head surpasses its original level. On the other hand, capital per head and income per head stay below their original levels, respectively. Consumption per head presumably ends up at a higher level. Figure 3.32 illuminates the trajectory of the deficit ratio, figure 3.33 reveals how public debt per head as well as capital per head develop over time, and figure 3.34 demonstrates the path of consumption per head. So far we talked about a tax cut. For a hike in the purchase ratio or a plunge in the saving ratio one could get very similar results.

6) Permanent tax cut ($s > \alpha$, $t < t'$). Under these circumstances, there will be no stationary equilibrium. At first the economy is in a stationary equilibrium with $t \geq t'$. The budget deficit and public debt, in per capita terms, do not change. Then suddenly the government reduces the tax rate below the critical level $t < t'$. In the phase diagram, the $\dot{d} = 0$ line is transposed to the right, whereas the $\dot{k} = 0$ line is transposed to the left, cf. figure 3.35. There exists no point of intersection any more. The streamline portrays the path along which the economy will move. In the short run, the tax cut improves consumption per head. And the ensuing jump in the deficit ratio deteriorates investment per head.

In the intermediate run, public debt per head swells round by round. By way of contrast, capital per head dwindles period by period. Beyond that, on account of the expansion in public debt per head, the government has to make more interest payments per head. This enlarges the deficit ratio, thus speeding up the expansion of public debt per head. As debt income per head mounts, so does consumption per head. In the long run, public debt per head grows without limits. This in turn drives capital per head down to zero. That means, the economy enters a vicious circle where the government raises loans in order to finance the interest payments on public debt. Figure 3.36 depicts the time path of the deficit ratio, and figure 3.37 exhibits the paths of public debt per head as well as capital per head.

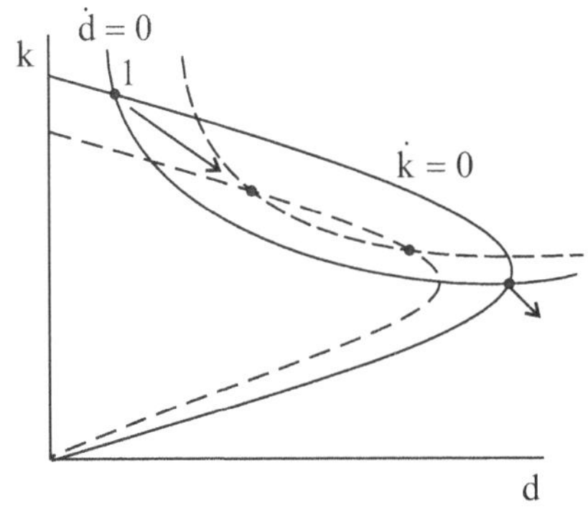

Figure 3.31
Permanent Tax Cut
($s > \alpha$, $t \geq t'$)

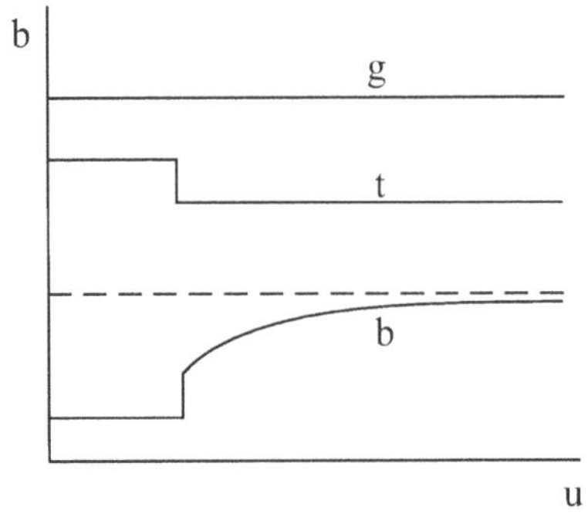

Figure 3.32
Permanent Tax Cut
($s > \alpha$, $t \geq t'$)

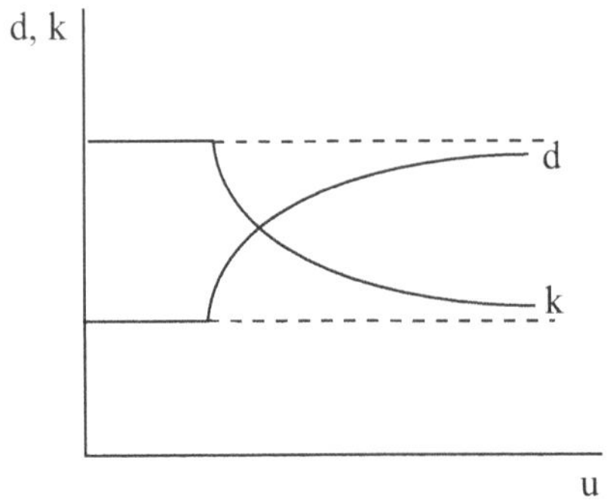

Figure 3.33
Permanent Tax Cut
($s > \alpha$, $t \geq t'$)

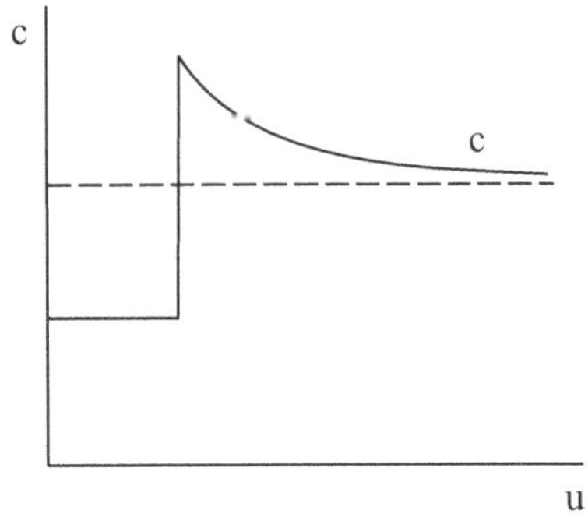

Figure 3.34
Permanent Tax Cut
($s > \alpha$, $t \geq t'$)

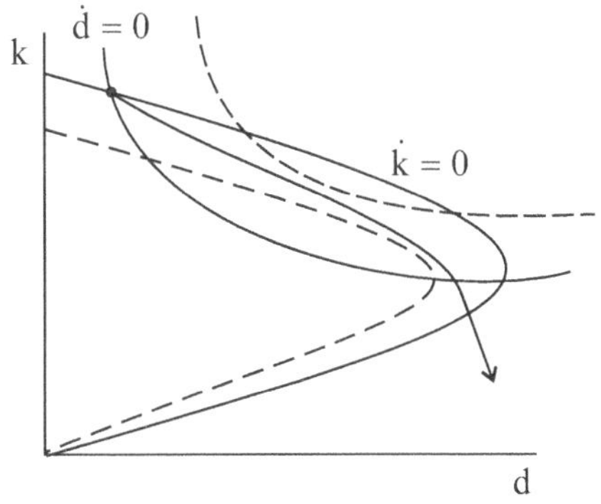

Figure 3.35
Permanent Tax Cut
($s > \alpha$, $t < t'$)

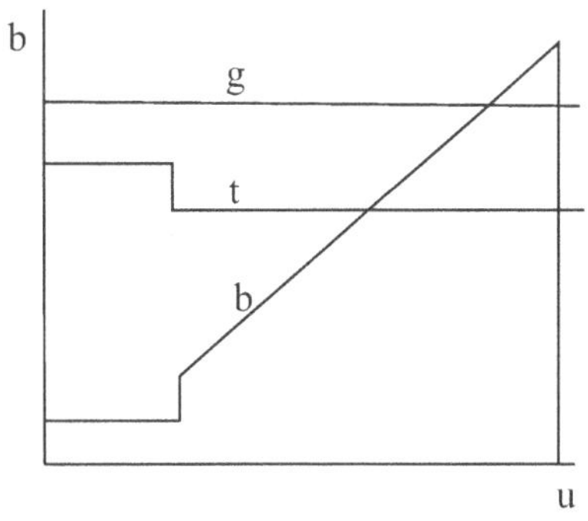

Figure 3.36
Permanent Tax Cut
($s > \alpha$, $t < t'$)

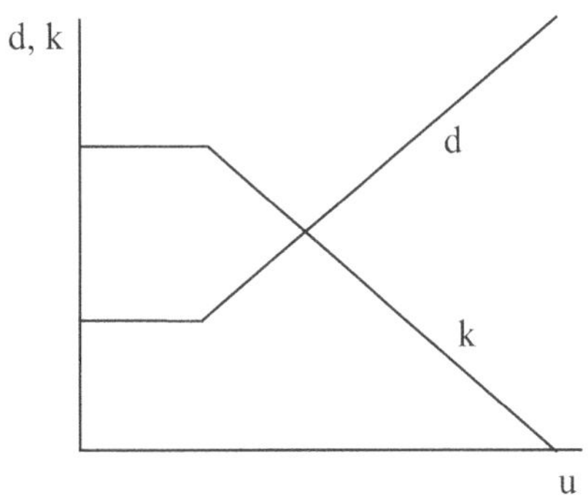

Figure 3.37
Permanent Tax Cut
($s > \alpha$, $t < t'$)

3.2.6 The Optimal Tax Rate

In the preceding sections, the tax rate was assumed to be given arbitrarily. In the current section, in place of that, we shall determine the optimal tax rate. The natural criterion for efficiency is the total of consumption and government purchases, in per capita terms respectively. Under the golden rule the interest rate coincides with the natural rate $r = n$. Accordingly the long-run equilibrium can be restated as:

$$y = k^{\alpha} \tag{1}$$

$$n = \alpha y / k \tag{2}$$

$$nd + nk = s(1 - t)(y + nd) \tag{3}$$

$$gy = t(y + nd) \tag{4}$$

Here d, k, t and y are endogenous. Eliminate nd in (3) by means of (4) and observe $n = \alpha y/k$ to arrive at the optimal tax rate:

$$t^* = \frac{(1 - s)g}{\beta - gs} \tag{5}$$

Clearly this is identical to the optimal tax rate deduced under a fixed deficit ratio. In the numerical example with $\beta = 0.8$, $g = 0.2$ and $s = 0.1$, the optimal tax rate is $t^* = 0.23$. Besides there exists a critical saving ratio:

$$s' = \alpha / (1 - g) \tag{6}$$

If $s \gtrless s'$, then $t^* \lessgtr g$. That is to say, under a high saving ratio, the optimal tax rate falls short of the purchase ratio. Conversely, under a low saving ratio, the optimal tax rate exceeds the purchase ratio. In the numerical example with $\alpha = 0.2$ and $g = 0.2$, the critical saving ratio is $s' = 0.25$. Last but not least, an increase in the purchase ratio brings up the optimal tax rate. How can this be made plausible? A rise in government purchases enlarges the budget deficit, thereby supplanting investment. To prevent undercapitalization, the government has to boost tax revenue.

3.2.7 The Optimal Saving Ratio

So far we started from the premise that the saving ratio is exogenous. Now we shall try to find out the saving ratio that maximizes the sum of consumption and government purchases per head. The long-run equilibrium is similar to the one obtained for the optimal tax rate. The only difference is that here d, k, s and y adjust themselves appropriately. This yields the optimal saving ratio:

$$s^* = \frac{g - \beta t}{(1-t)g} \tag{1}$$

Table 3.6 displays the optimal saving ratio as a function of the tax rate, based on the specification $\beta = 0.8$ and $g = 0.2$. In the real world, however, the saving ratio seems to stay close to $s = 0.1$.

Table 3.6
Tax Rate and Optimal Saving Ratio

t	s*
0.20	0.25
0.19	0.30
0.18	0.34
0.17	0.39
0.16	0.43
0.15	0.47

3.2.8 A Numerical Example

To illustrate this a bit more, have a look at a numerical example. It rests on the parameter values $\alpha = 0.2$, $g = 0.2$, $n = 0.03$ and $s = 0.4$. Table 3.7 reveals the long-run implications of a tax cut. In this instance, the saving ratio goes beyond the capital elasticity $s > \alpha$. So two cases are to be distinguished. If $t \geq 0.16$, there will be two long-run equilibria. Yet if $t < 0.16$, there will be no long-run equilibrium at all. Henceforth let be $t \geq 0.16$. In this situation, there exist two long-run equilibria, a stable one and an unstable one. Now regard the stable case. Then a reduction in the tax rate pushes up the deficit ratio, the interest rate and "consumption" per head. As opposed to that, it pulls down the capital-output ratio. By the way, the increase in consumption and government purchases per head is due to (heavy) overcapitalization.

Table 3.7
The Long-Run Effects of a Tax Cut

t	b	v	r	j
0.20	0	10.7	0.019	1.23
0.19	0.02	10.2	0.020	1.24
0.18	0.05	9.8	0.021	1.25
0.17	0.08	9.1	0.022	1.26
0.16	0.13	8.0	0.025	1.28
0.15	-	-	-	-

3.2.9 Summary

As a rule, there will be no long-run equilibrium. Starting from a balanced budget, a tax cut increases the deficit ratio, thereby reducing investment per head. In the long run, public debt per head tends to explode, which squeezes capital per head down to zero. As an exception, if the saving ratio is very high and if the primary deficit ratio is extremely low, there will be two long-run equilibria, a stable one and an unstable one.

Further there exists an optimal tax rate that maximizes the total of consumption and government purchases per head. Under a high saving ratio, the optimal tax rate falls short of the purchase ratio. Under a low saving ratio, on the other hand, the optimal tax rate exceeds the purchase ratio. As a fundamental result, a fixed tax rate generally cannot be sustained. This differs remarkably from the conclusions drawn for a fixed deficit ratio: A fixed deficit ratio generally can be sustained.

Of course the government can switch the regime. The government is free to choose between fixing the deficit ratio and fixing the tax rate. In other words, public choice decides on the existence and stability of the long-run equilibrium. The government is the master of sustainability, and not the victim of insustainability.

3.3 Fixing the Deficit Per Head

3.3.1 The Short-Run Equilibrium and the Long-Run Equilibrium

In section 3.1, we postulated that the government fixes the deficit ratio. In section 3.3, instead, we shall suppose that the government fixes the deficit per head. Let us begin with the dynamics of public debt. The government buys a certain volume of goods and services per head $G = gN$ with $g = const$. In addition the government borrows a given amount per capita $B = bN$ with $b = const$. The budget deficit in turn augments public debt $\dot{D} = B$. Apparently b denotes the deficit per head. Moreover the government collects a lumpsum tax $T = tN$ with $t = const$. The government pays the interest rate r on public debt D, so public interest equals rD. The government budget constraint is $B + T = G + rD$. Taking account of the functional relationships, the identity can be expressed as $bN + tN = gN + rD$. Here the government presets purchases per head and the deficit per head, while it adjusts the lumpsum tax.

We come next to capital dynamics. Factor income plus public interest minus tax load constitute disposable income $Y_d = Y + rD - T$. Households put aside a certain fraction of disposable income for saving purposes $S = sY_d$ with $s = const$. A part of savings is diverted by public borrowing, the rest going to investment $I = S - B$. Investment in turn adds to the stock of capital $\dot{K} = I$. Backward substitution provides $\dot{K} = s(Y + rD - T) - B$. Then note $B + T = G + rD$, $B = bN$ and $G = gN$ to reach $\dot{K} = s(Y + bN - gN) - bN$.

Having laid this foundation, the short-run equilibrium can be captured by a system of six equations:

$$Y = K^{\alpha} N^{\beta} \tag{1}$$

$$r = \alpha Y / K \tag{2}$$

$$\dot{K} = s(Y + bN - gN) - bN \tag{3}$$

$$\dot{D} = bN \tag{4}$$

$$bN + tN = gN + rD \tag{5}$$

$$\dot{N} = nN \tag{6}$$

Here r, t, $\dot{D}$, $\dot{K}$, $\dot{N}$ and Y are endogenous. Now it is convenient to reformulate the short-run equilibrium in per capita terms:

$$y = k^{\alpha} \tag{7}$$

$$r = \alpha y / k \tag{8}$$

$$\dot{k} = s(y + b - g) - b - nk \tag{9}$$

$$\dot{d} = b - nd \tag{10}$$

$$b + t = g + rd \tag{11}$$

Here $\dot{d}$, $\dot{k}$, r, t and y accommodate themselves.

In the steady state, the motion of public debt per head and of capital per head comes to a standstill $\dot{d} = 0$ and $\dot{k} = 0$. By virtue of that, the long-run equilibrium can be caught by a system of five equations:

$$y = k^{\alpha} \tag{12}$$

$$r = \alpha y / k \tag{13}$$

$$nk = s(y + b - g) - b \tag{14}$$

$$nd = b \tag{15}$$

$$b + t = g + rd \tag{16}$$

Here d, k, r, t and y are endogenous.

For the remainder of the current section we shall inquire into the relationship between the deficit per head and capital per head. Insert (12) into (14) to get $nk = s(k^{\alpha} + b - g) - b$. This equation determines capital per head. Unfortunately, however, it cannot be solved for k explicitly. In place of that it will be solved for b:

$$b = \frac{sk^{\alpha} - nk - gs}{1 - s} \tag{17}$$

Figure 3.38 visualizes the graph of this function. Evidently there is a critical deficit per head b', which gives rise to three cases. First, if b < b', there will be two long-run equilibria. Second, if b = b', there will be a unique long-run equilibrium. And third, if b > b', there will be no long-run equilibrium whatsoever.

Incidentally the critical deficit per head can be obtained in the following way. Differentiate (17) for k and set the derivative equal to zero, which furnishes:

$$k = (\alpha s / n)^{1/\beta} \tag{18}$$

Then put this term into (17) to gain the critical deficit per head. At last we ascertain the optimal deficit per head. Combine the golden rule r = n with (13) to realize:

$$k = (\alpha / n)^{1/\beta} \tag{19}$$

Then substitute this into (17) to achieve the desired purpose.

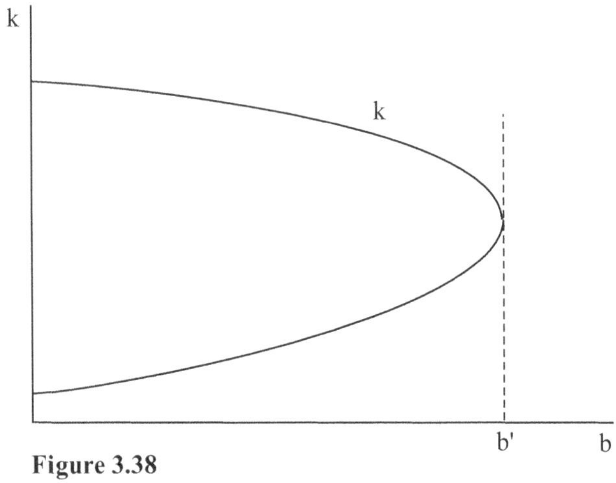

Figure 3.38
Deficit Per Head and Capital Per Head
(Solow Model)

3.3.2 Stability

The short-run equilibrium can be viewed as a system of two differential equations $\dot{d} = p(d, k)$ and $\dot{k} = q(d, k)$. At first we tackle the $\dot{d} = 0$ line. As a point of departure take

$$\dot{d} = b - nd \tag{1}$$

which is well known from the previous section. It is valid that $\partial\dot{d} / \partial d = -n < 0$. Then set $\dot{d} = 0$ and regroup:

$$d = b / n \tag{2}$$

Figure 3.40 presents the vertical $\dot{d} = 0$ line.

Now dispense with y in (9) from section 3.3.1 by making use of (7):

$$\dot{k} = s(k^{\alpha} + b - g) - b - nk \tag{3}$$

Figure 3.39 demonstrates how $\dot{k}$ varies with k. There exist two steady states k_1 and k_2 with $k_1 < k_2$, as can easily be seen. Correspondingly three cases can occur. First, if $k < k_1$, then $\dot{k} < 0$. Second, if $k_1 < k < k_2$, then $\dot{k} > 0$. And third, if $k_2 < k$, then $\dot{k} < 0$. As a corollary, the steady state k_1 proves to be unstable, while the steady state k_2 turns out to be stable.

Further set $\dot{k} = 0$ and reshuffle terms:

$$nk = s(k^{\alpha} + b - g) - b \tag{4}$$

Of course this reminds one of the long-run equilibrium, cf. section 3.3.1. In full analogy, there are two solutions $k_1 < k_2$. Figure 3.40 exhibits the horizontal $\dot{k} = 0$ lines. Taking all pieces together, figure 3.40 contains the phase diagram. To conclude, as long as the deficit per head stays below the critical level, there will be two long-run equilibria, one of them being stable, the other unstable. In this sense, a fixed deficit per head is feasible in the long run.

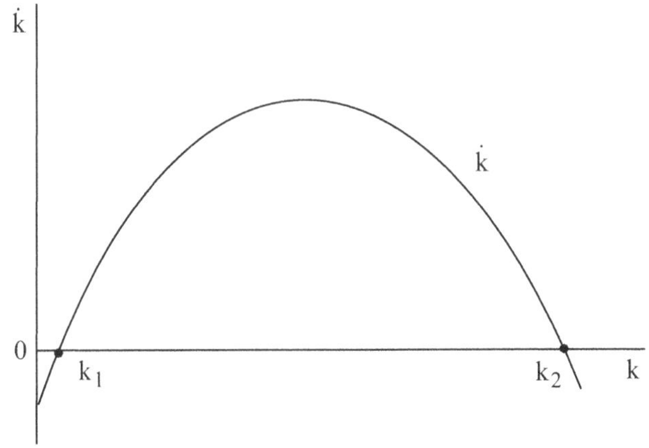

Figure 3.39
Fixed Deficit Per Head (Solow Model)

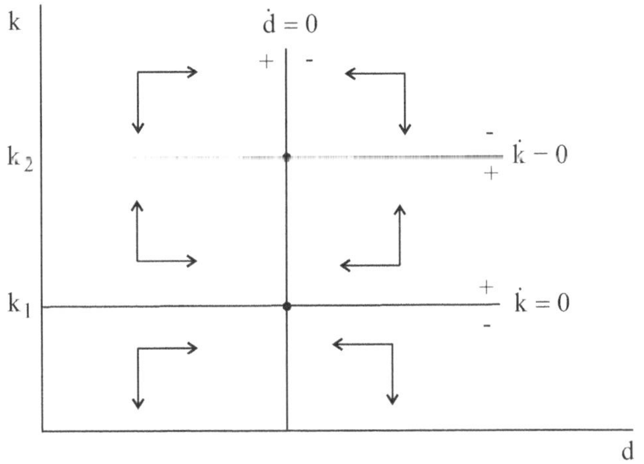

Figure 3.40
Fixed Deficit Per Head (Solow Model)

3.3.3 Some Shocks

Moreover we shall study the processes of adjustment kicked off by diverse shocks:

1) a permanent increase in the deficit per head ($b < b'$)
2) a permanent increase in the deficit per head ($b > b'$)
3) a transitory increase in the deficit per head ($b \lesseqgtr b'$)
4) an increase in government purchases per head ($b < b'$)
5) an increase in the natural rate of labour growth ($b < b'$)
6) an increase in the saving ratio ($b < b'$)

1) Permanent increase in the deficit per head ($b < b'$). In this situation there are two long-run equilibria, a stable one and an unstable one. Consider the stable case. At the beginning, the economy rests in the long-run equilibrium. The budget deficit and public debt, in per capita terms respectively, do not move. Investment per head and capital per head are uniform. Output, income and consumption per head stay put. Against this background, the government raises the deficit per head. In the phase diagram, the $\dot{d} = 0$ line shifts to the right, and the $\dot{k} = 0$ line shifts downwards, cf. figure 3.41. The streamline marks how the economy travels through time. In the short run, the disturbance lowers investment per head. According to the budget constraint, the government is able to reduce the lumpsum tax, thereby advancing consumption per head.

In the medium run, the rise in the deficit per head leads to the accumulation of public debt per head. The other way round, the fall in investment per head contributes to the decumulation of capital per head. As capital per head comes down, so do output, income and consumption per head. The building up of public debt per head, together with the surge in the interest rate, bring up public interest per head. Therefore the government must increase the lumpsum tax. Eventually the economy approaches a new long-run equilibrium. The budget deficit and public debt, in per capita terms respectively, do no longer move. Investment per head and capital per head have come to a halt. Output, income and consumption per head, too, have settled down. More precisely, public debt per head exceeds its pre-shock value, whereas capital per head falls short of its pre-shock value.

2) Permanent increase in the deficit per head ($b > b'$). In this condition there is no steady state. Initially let the economy reproduce itself in a steady state with $b < b'$. Public debt per head and capital per head are invariant. Then surprisingly the government lifts the deficit per head well above the critical level. In the short run, this action crowds out investment per head. In the intermediate run, public debt per head piles up round by round. That is why capital per head becomes dismantled period by period. As capital per head plummets, so do output, income, savings and investment per head. This in turn accelerates the depletion of capital per head, the economy enters a vicious circle. In the long run, capital per head shrinks back to zero. That means, there will be fatal crowding out. Ultimately the economy is bound to break down.

3) Transitory increase in the deficit per head ($b \lessgtr b'$). Under these circumstances there are two long-run equilibria, one of them being locally stable, the other unstable. Now select the locally stable case. Essentially the government can pursue three distinct strategies, cf. figure 3.42. Policy 1 is stable in a trivial way. Policy 2 is stable as well. But policy 3 is unstable. The effects of the alternative strategies on capital per head can be learnt from figure 3.43. With policy 3, the economy has passed the point of no return. During transition, capital per head has become too small. Inevitably the economy must collapse.

4) Increase in government purchases per head ($b < b'$). In this situation there are two long-run equilibria. Choose the stable case. At the start the economy is in the long-run equilibrium. Public debt per head and capital per head do not change. Then abruptly the government pushes up its purchases per head. In the phase diagram, the $\dot{k} = 0$ line is transposed downwards, cf. figure 3.44. In the short run, the government has to enhance the lumpsum tax, so savings per head and investment per head are discouraged. In the medium run, because of the drop in investment per head, capital per head declines step by step. The budget deficit per head is constant, however, hence public debt per head remains unaffected. In due course the economy tends to a new long-run equilibrium. Capital per head does not change any more. Properly speaking, public debt per head did not stir at all, while capital per head descended to a lower level.

5) Increase in the natural rate of labour growth ($b < b'$). Regard the stable case. Originally the economy is in the stationary equilibrium. Public debt per head and capital per head hold fast. Then spontaneously labour growth speeds

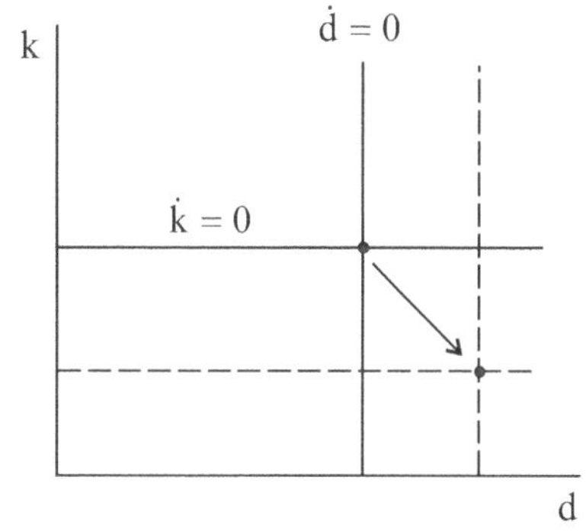

Figure 3.41
Permanent Increase in
Deficit Per Head (b < b')

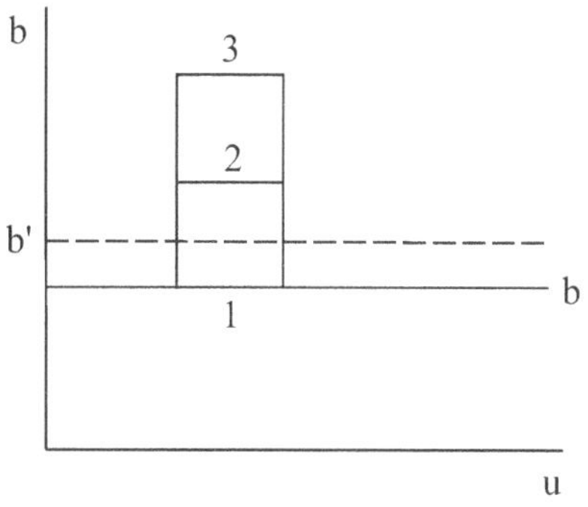

Figure 3.42
Transitory Increase in
Deficit Per Head $(b \lesseqgtr b')$

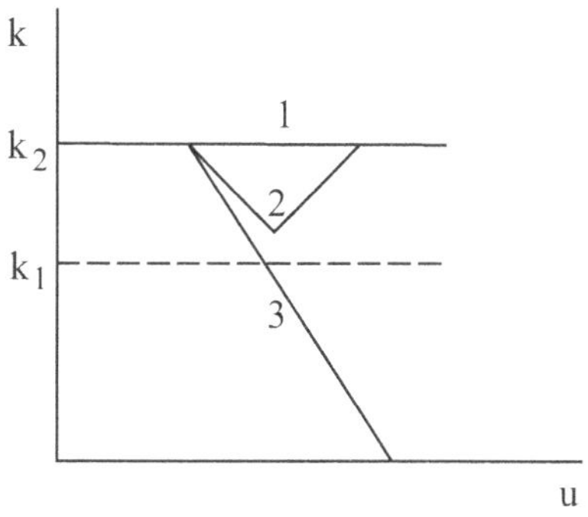

Figure 3.43
Transitory Increase in
Deficit Per Head $(b \lesseqgtr b')$

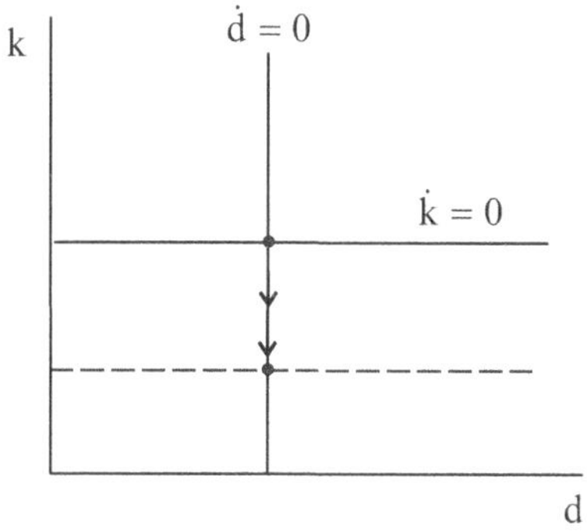

Figure 3.44
Increase in Purchases Per Head

up. In the phase diagram, the $\dot{d} = 0$ line wanders to the left, and the $\dot{k} = 0$ line wanders downwards, cf. figure 3.45. In the short run, as measured by the growth rate, labour expands faster than capital, thus depressing capital per head. Likewise labour expands more rapidly than public debt, so public debt per head diminishes. With the lapse of time the economy reaches a new stationary equilibrium. Both public debt per head and capital per head settle down at deeper levels.

6) Increase in the saving ratio ($b < b'$). Take the stable case. At the beginning the economy reproduces itself in the steady state. Public debt per head and capital per head are uniform. Then autonomously the saving ratio springs up. In the phase diagram, the $\dot{k} = 0$ line glides upwards, cf. figure 3.46. In the short run, the disruption elevates savings per head and investment per head. In the intermediate run, capital per head piles up. Asymptotically the economy converges to a new steady state. Public debt per head did not vary during the process, and capital per head climbed to a superior level.

3.3.4 Summary

The investigation furnishes a critical deficit per head. As long as the deficit per head falls short of the critical value, there will be two long-run equilibria, a stable one and an unstable one. But as soon as the deficit per head exceeds the critical value, there will be no long-run equilibrium at all. Put another way, under a low deficit per head, an increase in the deficit per head reduces capital per head to a certain extent. On the other hand, under a high deficit per head, a further increase drives capital per head down to zero. That means, an infinitely small cause can have quite large an effect. As an outcome, a fixed deficit per head generally can be sustained.

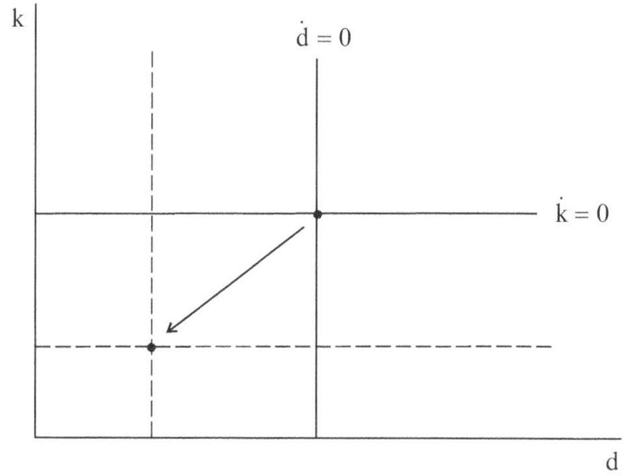

Figure 3.45
Increase in Labour Growth

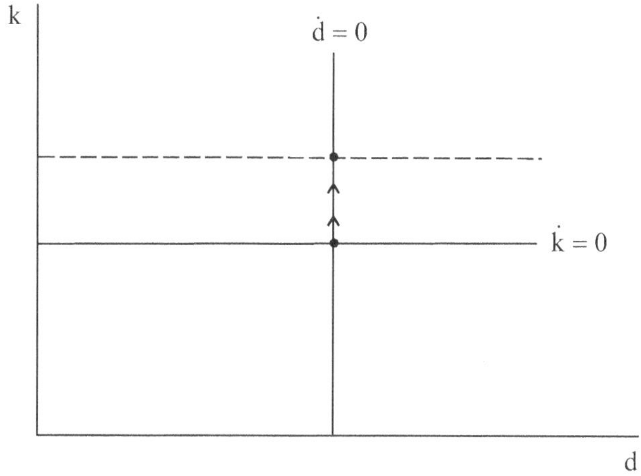

Figure 3.46
Increase in Saving Ratio

3.4 Fixing the Tax Per Head

3.4.1 The Short-Run Equilibrium and the Long-Run Equilibrium

In section 3.2, we assumed that the government fixes the tax rate. In section 3.4, instead, we shall postulate that the government fixes the tax per head. Let us begin with budget dynamics. The government spends a certain per capita amount on goods and services $G = gN$ with $g = \text{const}$. In addition the government imposes a lumpsum tax $T = tN$ with $t = \text{const}$. The budget deficit can be defined as the excess of government purchases and public interest over tax revenue $B = G + rD - T$. The budget deficit augments public debt $\dot{D} = B$. This involves $\dot{D} = gN + rD - tN$.

Next have a look at investment dynamics. Factor income plus public interest minus tax load make up disposable income $Y_d = Y + rD - T$. Households save a given proportion of disposable income $S = sY_d$ with $s = \text{const}$. A good deal of savings is absorbed by public borrowing, the remainder being left for investment $I = S - B$. Investment in turn adds to the stock of capital $\dot{K} = I$. From this one can infer $\dot{K} = s(Y + rD - T) - B$. Pay heed to $T = tN$ as well as $\dot{D} = B$ and rearrange $\dot{D} + \dot{K} = s(Y + rD - tN)$

Therefore the short-run equilibrium can be encapsulated in a system of five equations:

$$Y = K^{\alpha} N^{\beta} \tag{1}$$

$$r = \alpha Y / K \tag{2}$$

$$\dot{D} + \dot{K} = s(Y + rD - tN) \tag{3}$$

$$\dot{D} = gN + rD - tN \tag{4}$$

$$\dot{N} = nN \tag{5}$$

Here r, $\dot{D}$, $\dot{K}$, $\dot{N}$ and Y are endogenous. Again it is necessary to conduct the analysis in per capita terms:

$$y = k^{\alpha} \tag{6}$$

$$r = \alpha y / k \tag{7}$$

$$\dot{d} + \dot{k} = s(y + rd - t) - nd - nk \tag{8}$$

$$\dot{d} = g + rd - t - nd \tag{9}$$

Here $\dot{d}$, $\dot{k}$, r and y adapt themselves.

In the steady state, public debt per head and capital per head stop to adjust $\dot{d} = \dot{k} = 0$. For that reason the long-run equilibrium can be enshrined in a system of four equations:

$$y = k^{\alpha} \tag{10}$$

$$r = \alpha y / k \tag{11}$$

$$nd + nk = s(y + rd - t) \tag{12}$$

$$nd = g + rd - t \tag{13}$$

In this version d, k, r and y accommodate themselves.

3.4.2 Stability

The short-run equilibrium can be interpreted as a system of two differential equations $\dot{d} = p(d, k)$ and $\dot{k} = q(d, k)$. At first we address the $\dot{d} = 0$ line. As a starting point consider

$$\dot{d} = g + rd - t - nd \tag{1}$$

from the previous section. If $r \lesseqgtr n$, then $\partial\dot{d} / \partial d \lesseqgtr 0$. Also note $r = \alpha k^{-\beta}$ to get:

$$\dot{d} = g + \alpha d k^{-\beta} - t - nd \tag{2}$$

The assessment of (2) gives rise to a critical value of capital per head $k' = (\alpha / n)^{1/\beta}$. If $k \lesseqgtr k'$, then $\partial\dot{d} / \partial d \gtreqless 0$. Further set $\dot{d} = 0$ to gain:

$$d = \frac{g - t}{n - r} \tag{3}$$

Henceforth let be $t < g$. Thus two cases emerge from the evaluation of (3). If the interest rate stays below the natural rate, public debt per head will be positive. Conversely, if the interest rate surpasses the natural rate, public debt per head will be negative. The second case appears to conflict with the assumptions, so one may guess that a long-run equilibrium does not exist. On that grounds let the interest rate be smaller than the natural rate, hence public debt per head will be positive. What is more, public debt per head tends to infinity as the interest rate comes close to the natural rate. Moreover get rid of r in (3) with the help of $r = \alpha k^{-\beta}$:

$$d = \frac{g - t}{n - \alpha k^{-\beta}} \tag{4}$$

That means, an increase in k correlates with a decline in d. Beyond that, d converges to $(g - t)/n$ as k becomes very large. Having laid this groundwork, we can draw the negatively inclined $\dot{d} = 0$ line in figure 3.47.

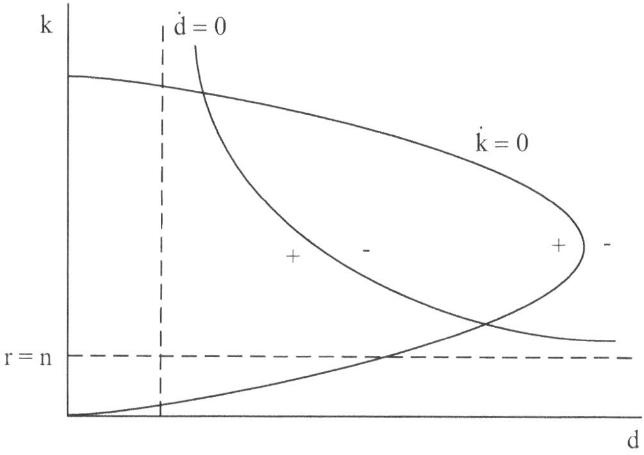

Figure 3.47
Fixed Tax Per Head
(Solow Model)

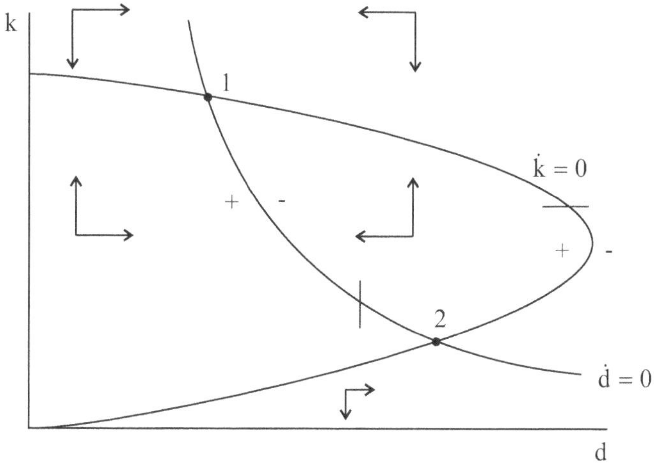

Figure 3.48
Fixed Tax Per Head
(Solow Model)

At this junction, we leave the $\dot{d} = 0$ line and turn to the $\dot{k} = 0$ line. Equations (6) to (9) from the foregoing section imply:

$$\dot{k} = sk^{\alpha} + (1-s)t - g - (1-s)\alpha dk^{-\beta} - nk \tag{5}$$

By the way it applies $\partial\dot{k} / \partial d < 0$. Then set $\dot{k} = 0$ and solve for d:

$$d = \frac{sk^{\alpha} + (1-s)t - g - nk}{(1-s)\alpha k^{-\beta}} \tag{6}$$

Correspondingly figure 3.47 illuminates the $\dot{k} = 0$ line.

Over and above that, assembling all component parts, figure 3.48 offers the phase diagram. The lesson taught by the phase diagram is that there are two long-run equilibria $k_1 > k_2$, the first being stable, the second unstable.

3.4.3 A Tax Cut

Let be $t < g$. Against this background, there exists a critical tax per head t'. If $s < \alpha$ or $t < t'$, there will be no long-run equilibrium. By way of contrast, if $s > \alpha$ and $t \geq t'$, there will in fact be a long-run equilibrium. This can be proved along the same lines as in section 3.2.3. In the current section, we shall keep track of the process set in motion by a permanent tax cut. In doing this, we distinguish between two cases:

1) $s < \alpha$ and $t < g$
2) $s > \alpha$ and $t \geq t'$

1) Permanent tax cut ($s < \alpha$, $t < g$). In this situation there exists no long-run equilibrium. At the beginning, the economy rests in a long-run equilibrium with $t = g$. The budget is balanced $b = 0$, so there is no public debt $d = 0$. Investment per head and capital per head do not move. Under these circumstances, the government reduces the lumpsum tax. In the short run, this action brings the budget into deficit, thereby curbing investment per head. In the medium run, public debt per head is heaped up. As opposed to that, capital per head is run down. Further, on account of the expansion in public debt per head, the government has to disburse more interest payments per head. This enlarges the budget deficit, thus speeding up the expansion of public debt, in per capita terms, respectively. In the long run, public debt per head proliferates without bounds. This in turn squeezes capital per head down to zero. Put differently, there will be fatal crowding out. Public debt acts like a killer virus, it breeds on itself and displaces all other activities.

2) Permanent tax cut ($s > \alpha$, $t \geq t'$). In this condition, there are two long-run equilibria, a stable one and an unstable one. Contemplate the stable case. Initially the economy reproduces itself in the steady number one, cf. figure 3.31 in section 3.2.5. Public debt per head and capital per head do not vary. Then, all of a sudden, the government lowers the lumpsum tax. In the phase diagram, the $\dot{d} = 0$ line shifts to the right, while the $\dot{k} = 0$ line shifts to the left. In the short run, the government must raise the deficit per head, which puts a brake on investment per head. In the intermediate run, public debt per head accumulates. That is why capital per head becomes dismantled. With the lapse of time, the economy draws near another steady state. Public debt per head and capital per head stop to adjust.

More precisely, public debt per head lies above its original level, whereas capital per head lies below.

3.4.4 Summary

As a rule, there will be no long-run equilibrium. A reduction in the lumpsum tax increases the deficit per head, thereby curtailing investment per head. In the long run, public debt per head grows without limits, so capital per head shrinks back to zero. As an exception, if the saving ratio is very high and if the primary deficit per head is extremely low, there will be two long-run equilibria, a stable one and an unstable one. As a finding, a fixed tax per head generally cannot be sustained. Compare this to a fixed deficit per head, which is feasible in the long run.

4 Overlapping Generations

4.1 Fixing the Deficit Ratio

4.1.1 The Short-Run Equilibrium

At this stage, we leave the Solow model and turn to the overlapping generations model. The Solow model was based on a fixed saving ratio. The overlapping generations model, instead, assumes intertemporal optimization by private agents within a finite horizon.

Firms manufacture a single commodity Y by making use of capital K and labour N. For the sake of simplicity, let technology be of the Cobb-Douglas type $Y = K^{\alpha}N^{\beta}$, exhibiting constant returns to scale $\alpha > 0$, $\beta > 0$, $\alpha + \beta = 1$. More exactly, N denotes the number of active workers. Each worker has got a job. Output can be dedicated to consumption, investment and government purchases $Y = C + I + G$. Firms maximize profits $\Pi = Y - rK - wN$ under perfect competition. Therefore the interest rate corresponds to the marginal product of capital $r = \alpha Y/K$. Analogously the wage rate coincides with the marginal product of labour $w = \beta Y/N$.

Now we come to the dynamics of public debt. The government spends a given proportion of national income on goods and services $G = gY$ with $g =$ const. Moreover the government borrows a specified fraction of national income $B = bY$ with $b =$ const. Public debt this period plus the budget deficit this period add up to public debt next period $D_{+1} = D + B$. The government pays the interest rate r on public debt D, so public interest amounts to rD. The government levies a tax at the flat rate t on factor income and debt income $T = t(Y + rD)$. The government budget constraint is $B + T = G + rD$. Take account of the functional relationships to see $bY + t(Y + rD) = gY + rD$. Here the government presets the purchase ratio and the deficit ratio, while it must adapt the tax rate suitably.

Further the limelight will be directed at capital dynamics. The individual life-cycle is composed of two periods, of the working period and of the retirement period. During the working period, the individual receives labour income, which he partly consumes and partly saves. The savings are used to buy government bonds and private bonds. During the retirement period, the individual earns interest on the bonds and sells the bonds altogether. The proceeds are entirely consumed, no bequests are left.

The utility u of the representative individual depends on consumption per head in the working period c^1 and on consumption per head in the retirement period c^2. Take a logarithmic utility function:

$$u = \gamma \log c^1 + \delta \log c^2 \tag{1}$$

with $\gamma > 0$, $\delta > 0$ and $\gamma + \delta = 1$. We postulate that government purchases do not affect intertemporal allocation. That means, government purchases do not enter the utility function explicitly.

The budget constraint of the representative individual covers the whole lifecycle. $(1 - t)w$ is net labour income in the working period and $(1 - t)w - c^1$ are savings in the working period. The individual earns the net interest rate $(1 - t)r$ on savings, so consumption in the retirement period is $[(1 - t)w - c^1][1 + (1 - t)r] = c^2$. As a consequence, the individual budget constraint can be stated as:

$$c^1 + \frac{c^2}{1+(1-t)r} = (1-t)w \tag{2}$$

The individual chooses present and future consumption so as to maximize utility subject to his budget constraint. The evaluation of the Lagrange function yields consumption per head in the working period $c^1 = (1-t)\gamma w$. Net labour income minus consumption per head gives savings per head $s = (1 - t)w - c^1$ or $s = (1 - t)\delta w$. The savings of the active generation amount to $S = sN$. Observe $s = (1 - t)\delta w$ and $w = \beta Y/N$ to arrive at $S = (1 - t)\beta\delta Y$. The savings of the young generation serve to finance public debt and private capital of the subsequent period $D_{+1} + K_{+1} = S$. From this one can infer $D_{+1} + K_{+1} = (1 - t)\beta\delta Y$. Besides let labour grow at the natural rate $N_{+1} = (1+n)N$.

On this foundation, the short-run equilibrium can be represented by a system of six equations:

$$Y = K^{\alpha} N^{\beta} \tag{3}$$

$$r = \alpha Y / K \tag{4}$$

$$D_{+1} + K_{+1} = (1 - t)\beta\delta Y \tag{5}$$

$$D_{+1} = D + bY \tag{6}$$

$$bY + t(Y + rD) = gY + rD \tag{7}$$

$$N_{+1} = (1 + n)N \tag{8}$$

Here α, β, δ, b, g, n, D, K and N are exogenous, whereas r, t, D_{+1}, K_{+1}, N_{+1} and Y are endogenous.

It is convenient to do the research in per capita terms. Divide (5) through by N to reach:

$$\frac{D_{+1}}{N_{+1}} \frac{N_{+1}}{N} + \frac{K_{+1}}{N_{+1}} \frac{N_{+1}}{N} = \frac{(1-t)\beta\delta Y}{N} \tag{9}$$

Paying heed to (8), this can be written as $(1+n)d_{+1} + (1+n)k_{+1} = (1-t)\beta\delta y$. For instance, y = Y/N stands for income per head of the young. In this way, the short-run equilibrium can be encapsulated in a system of five equations:

$$y = k^{\alpha} \tag{10}$$

$$r = \alpha y / k \tag{11}$$

$$(1+n)d_{+1} + (1+n)k_{+1} = (1-t)\beta\delta y \tag{12}$$

$$(1+n)d_{+1} = d + by \tag{13}$$

$$by + t(y + rd) = gy + rd \tag{14}$$

Here d_{+1}, k_{+1}, r, t and y accommodate themselves.

4.1.2 The Long-Run Equilibrium

In the steady state, the motion of public debt per head and of capital per head comes to a standstill: $d_{+1} = d$ and $k_{+1} = k$. Accordingly the long-run equilibrium can be formulated as a system of five equations:

$$y = k^{\alpha} \tag{1}$$

$$r = \alpha y / k \tag{2}$$

$$(1 + n)d + (1 + n)k = (1 - t)\beta\delta y \tag{3}$$

$$nd = by \tag{4}$$

$$by + t(y + rd) = gy + rd \tag{5}$$

In this condition d, k, r, t and y are endogenous.

Beyond that we shall derive the steady state values of capital per head and of the capital-output ratio, respectively. At first solve (5) for $1 - t = (1 + b - g)/(1 + rd/y)$. Then dispense with y in (4) by means of (1) to accomplish $d = bk^{\alpha} / n$. This together with (2) and (1) provides $rd / y = \alpha b / nk^{\beta}$. Insert this into $1 - t = (1 + b - g)/(1 + rd/y)$ to get:

$$1 - t = \frac{1 + b - g}{1 + \alpha b / nk^{\alpha}} \tag{6}$$

Finally put this in conjunction with $d = bk^{\alpha} / n$ and $y = k^{\alpha}$ into (3) and regroup:

$$(1 + n)bk^{\alpha} / n + (1 + n)k = \frac{(1 + b - g)\beta\delta k}{k^{\beta} + \alpha b / n} \tag{7}$$

This equation determines capital per head. By virtue $v = k^{\beta}$, (7) can be restated as follows:

$$(1 + n)\alpha b^2 / n^2 + (1 + n)v^2 = \left[(1 + b - g)\beta\delta - (1 + n)(1 + \alpha)b / n\right]v \tag{8}$$

Here $v = k/y$ symbolizes the capital-output ratio. Evidently (8) is a quadratic equation in v, furnishing two solutions.

To illustrate this, consider a numerical example with $\alpha = 0.2$, $\delta = 0.4$, $g = 0.2$ and $n = 1.427$. The last item corresponds to an annual growth rate of 3% over a period of 30 years. Table 4.1 reveals the capital-output ratio as a function of the deficit ratio. Strictly speaking, there are two long-run equilibria. An increase in b lowers v_1, which matches the results obtained in the Solow model. On the other hand, an increase in b raises v_2. This seems to be quite paradoxical, suggesting that the second steady state will be unstable.

Table 4.1
Deficit Ratio and Capital-Output Ratio

b	v_1	v_2
0	0.105	
0.01	0.098	0.0001
0.02	0.091	0.0004
0.03	0.083	0.001

4.1.3 Stability

The short-run equilibrium can be compressed to a system of two difference equations:

$$d_{+1} = p(d,k) \tag{1}$$

$$k_{+1} = q(d,k) \tag{2}$$

To begin with, we shall ascertain equation (1). Combine $(1+n)d_{+1} = d + by$ and $y = k^{\alpha}$:

$$d_{+1} = \frac{d + bk^{\alpha}}{1+n} \tag{3}$$

As a corollary we have $\partial d_{+1} / \partial d = 1/(1+n) < 1$. Next the dd boundary line will be introduced, being defined by $d_{+1} = d$:

$$d = bk^{\alpha} / n \tag{4}$$

Figure 4.1 displays the upward sloping dd line.

Moreover we shall try to find out equation (2). (12) from section 4.1.1 in conjunction with (13) and (10) yields:

$$(1+n)k_{+1} = (1-t)\beta\delta k^{\alpha} - d - bk^{\alpha} \tag{5}$$

In addition solve (14) from section 4.1.1 for 1 – t and note (11):

$$1-t = \frac{1+b-g}{1+\alpha d/k} \tag{6}$$

Further eliminate 1 – t in (5) by means of (6) to check:

$$(1+n)k_{+1} = \frac{(1+b-g)\beta\delta k^{\alpha}}{1+\alpha d/k} - d - bk^{\alpha} \tag{7}$$

Apparently it holds $\partial k_{+1} / \partial d < 0$. At last set $k_{+1} = k$ to verify the equation of the kk boundary line:

$$d + bk^{\alpha} + (1+n)k = \frac{(1+b-g)\beta\delta k^{\alpha}}{1+\alpha d/k} \tag{8}$$

At the point k = 0, d vanishes. And for d = 0, (8) simplifies to:

$$k^{\beta} = \frac{(1+b-g)\beta\delta - b}{1+n} \tag{9}$$

Thus figure 4.1 portrays the backward bending kk line.

Judging from the phase diagram, there exist two long-run equilibria $k_1 > k_2$, the first being stable, the second unstable. The process of adjustment is structurally identical to that discussed in the Solow model. As a conclusion, a fixed deficit ratio generally can be sustained.

4.1.4 Summary

The analysis gives rise to a critical deficit ratio. If the deficit ratio falls short of the critical level, there will be two long-run equilibria, a stable one and an unstable one. If the deficit ratio exceeds the critical level, however, there will be no long-run equilibrium. Under a low deficit ratio, an increase in the deficit ratio reduces capital per head. But under a high deficit ratio, an increase in the deficit ratio forces capital per head down to zero. In this sense, a fixed deficit ratio generally can be sustained.

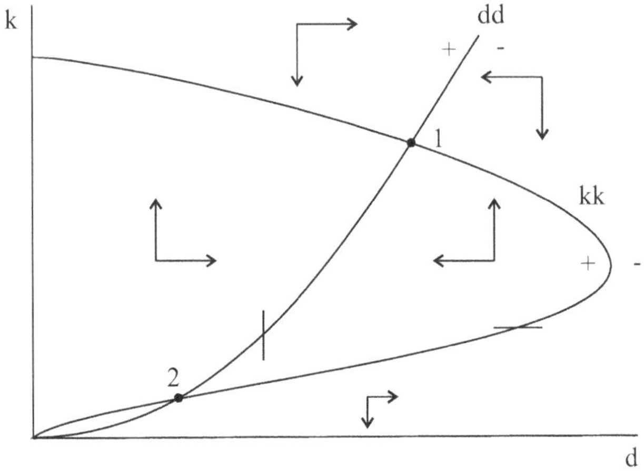

Figure 4.1
Fixed Deficit Ratio
(Overlapping Generations)

4.2 Fixing the Tax Rate

4.2.1 The Short-Run Equilibrium

We start right out with budget dynamics. The government buys a certain fraction of national product $G = gY$ with $g = const.$ In addition the government collects a proportionate tax on both factor income and debt income $T = t(Y + rD)$ with $t = const.$ The budget deficit registers the difference between government expenditures and tax proceeds $B = G + rD - T$. Public debt this period plus the budget deficit this period add up to public debt next period $D_{+1} = D + B$. From this follows $D_{+1} = D + gY + rD - t(Y + rD)$.

Apart from this we pursue the same approach as in section 4.1.1. Thus the short-run equilibrium can be characterized by a system of five equations:

$$Y = K^{\alpha} N^{\beta} \tag{1}$$

$$r = \alpha Y / K \tag{2}$$

$$D_{+1} + K_{+1} = (1 - t)\beta\delta Y \tag{3}$$

$$D_{+1} = D + gY + rD - t(Y + rD) \tag{4}$$

$$N_{+1} = (1 + n)N \tag{5}$$

Here α, β, δ, g, n, t, D, K and N are exogenous, while r, D_{+1}, K_{+1}, N_{+1} and Y are endogenous. Moreover it is suitable to restate this in per capita terms:

$$y = k^{\alpha} \tag{6}$$

$$r = \alpha y / k \tag{7}$$

$$(1 + n)d_{+1} + (1 + n)k_{+1} = (1 - t)\beta\delta y \tag{8}$$

$$(1 + n)d_{+1} = d + gy + rd - t(y + rd) \tag{9}$$

In this version d_{+1}, k_{+1}, r and y adjust themselves appropriately.

4.2.2 The Long-Run Equilibrium

In the steady state, public debt per head and capital per head cease to move $d_{+1} = d$ and $k_{+1} = k$. By virtue of that, the long-run equilibrium can be expressed as a system of four equations:

$$y = k^{\alpha} \quad (1)$$

$$r = \alpha y / k \quad (2)$$

$$(1+n)d + (1+n)k = (1-t)\beta\delta y \quad (3)$$

$$nd = gy + rd - t(y + rd) \quad (4)$$

Here d, k, r and y adapt themselves.

In the main part of this section, we shall diagnose the condition for the existence of a steady state. The proof draws heavily on Michaelis (1989). At first rephrase (2) as $rd = \alpha xy$, where $x = d/k$ denotes the debt-capital ratio that emerges as a strategic variable. Moreover install the primary deficit ratio $h = g - t$. Paying attention to this, (4) can be written as:

$$nd = hy + (1-t)\alpha xy \quad (5)$$

Further divide (3) by (5) and reshuffle:

$$\frac{(1+n)(1+x)}{nx} = \frac{(1-t)\beta\delta}{h + (1-t)\alpha x} \quad (6)$$

This is a quadratic equation in x, as can readily be seen. Henceforth, to avoid needless complexity, we posit $t = 0$, which involves $h = g$. In other words, can the government provide goods and services without imposing a tax? Now solve (6) for x:

$$x = -\frac{(\alpha+g)(1+n) - \beta\delta n}{2\alpha(1+n)} \pm \sqrt{\left[\frac{(\alpha+g)(1+n) - \beta\delta n}{2\alpha(1+n)}\right]^2 - \frac{g}{\alpha}} \quad (7)$$

The reduced discriminant $U = [(\alpha + g)(1 + n) - \beta\delta n]^2 - 4\alpha g(1 + n)^2$ becomes zero at

$$g_{1,2} = \alpha + \frac{\beta\delta n}{1+n} \mp \sqrt{\frac{4\alpha\beta\delta n}{1+n}} \tag{8}$$

The examination of (8) shows that g_1 and g_2 are both real and positive with $g_1 < g_2$. x in turn is real and positive if and only if

$$\delta > \alpha(1+n)/\beta n \text{ and } g \leq g_1 \tag{9}$$

The proof can be found in the appendix to this section. That is to say, a long-run equilibrium does exist if and only if the future consumption elasticity is high and the government purchase ratio is low. As a principal result, this is the necessary and sufficient condition for a fixed tax rate $t = 0$ to be feasible in the long-run.

To better understand this, contemplate a numerical example with $\alpha = 0.2$ and $n = 1.427$ (i. e. an annual growth of 3% extending over 30 years). Table 4.2 indicates the maximum purchase ratio that can be sustained. If $\delta = 0.3$ or $\delta = 0.4$, then $g_1 = 0$. Of course, a purchase ratio of zero will be feasible in the long run. By way of contrast, a purchase ratio greater than zero will not be feasible. Beyond that, if $\delta = 0.5$, which means no discount of future consumption, then $g_1 = 0.001$. Here two cases have to be distinguished. As long as the purchase ratio stays below 0.001, it will be feasible in the long run. Yet as soon as it surpasses 0.001, it will not be feasible any more. How can these findings be transferred to an environment with a tax rate of $t = 0.2$? Let be $\delta = 0.5$. Then, presumably, a tax rate exceeding 0.199 can be sustained. As opposed to that, a tax rate falling short of 0.199 cannot be sustained.

From the empirical point of view, a fixed tax rate appears not to be feasible in the long run. On the other hand, there may be an exception to this rule. If both the future consumption elasticity is very high and the primary deficit ratio is extremely low, then a fixed tax rate indeed is feasible. Essentially this underlines the importance of the conclusions drawn in the Solow model.

Table 4.2
Maximum Sustainable Purchase Ratio

δ	g_1
0.1	0
0.2	0
0.3	0
0.4	0
0.5	0.001
0.6	0.007
0.7	0.016

Appendix

Evidently (7) can be written as $x = -P/Q \pm \sqrt{R}$. In addition, the reduced discriminant of (7) can be stated as $U = (h - h_1)(h - h_2)$. This gives rise to four cases. First, if $g_1 < g < g_2$, then $U < 0$. Second, if $g \leq g_1$ and $\delta < \alpha(1 + n)/\beta n$, then $U \geq 0$ and $x < 0$. Proof: P is positive. Now square $\sqrt{R} < P/Q$ to confirm $x < 0$. Third, if $g \leq g_1$ and $\delta > \alpha(1 + n)/\beta n$, then $U \geq 0$ and $x > 0$. In this case, P is negative. Next square $-P/Q > \sqrt{R}$ to verify $x > 0$. Fourth, if $g \geq g_2$, then $U \geq 0$ and $x < 0$. Proof: Here P is positive. Finally square $\sqrt{R} < P/Q$ to see $x < 0$.

4.2.3 Stability

In the current section, we return to an economy with taxation. The short-run equilibrium can be condensed to a system of two difference equations $d_{+1} = p(d, k)$ and $k_{+1} = g(d, k)$. Let us begin with $d_{+1} = p(d, k)$. Get rid of y in (9) by applying (6) from section 4.2.1, respectively:

$$(1+n)d_{+1} = d + gk^{\alpha} + (1-t)rd - tk^{\alpha} \quad (1)$$

If $(1 - t)r \lesseqgtr n$, then $\partial d_{+1}/\partial d \lesseqgtr 1$, as can be learnt from (1). Now take account of $r = \alpha y/k$, which leads to a critical level of capital per head:

$$k' = [(1-t)\alpha / n]^{1/\beta} \quad (2)$$

In the same vein, if $k \lesseqgtr k'$, then $\partial d_{+1}/\partial d \gtreqless 1$.

Further set $d_{+1} = d$ and rearrange:

$$d = \frac{(g-t)k^{\alpha}}{n-(1-t)r} \quad (3)$$

Let $t < g$. According to (3), two cases can occur. If $(1 - t)r < n$, then $d > 0$. Conversely, if $(1 - t)r > n$, then $d < 0$. This seems to be inconsistent, so one may suspect that in this case a long-run equilibrium does not exist. Henceforth we posit $(1 - t)r < n$, which implies $d > 0$. Public debt per head tends to infinity as the net interest rate converges to the natural rate from below. Besides insert $r = \alpha k^{-\beta}$ into (3):

$$d = \frac{(g-t)k}{nk^{\beta} - (1-t)\alpha} \quad (4)$$

Owing to (4), if capital per head grows without limits, so does public debt per head. Figure 4.2 visualizes the forward bending dd line, which is reminiscent of the Solow model.

Next have a look at $k_{+1} = q(d, k)$. Substitute (9) into (8) from section 4.2.1, respectively, and observe $y = k^{\alpha}$ as well as $r = \alpha y/k$:

$$(1+n)k_{+1} = [(1-t)\beta\delta + t - g]k^{\alpha} - [1+(1-t)\alpha k^{-\beta}]d \qquad (5)$$

Obviously it holds $\partial k_{+1} / \partial d < 0$. Beyond that set $k_{+1} = k$ and solve for d:

$$d = \frac{[(1-t)\beta\delta + t - g]k^{\alpha} - (1+n)k}{1+(1-t)\alpha k^{-\beta}} \qquad (6)$$

Figure 4.2 illuminates the backward bending kk line, too. For d = 0, equation (6) yields:

$$k'' = \left[\frac{(1-t)\beta\delta + t - g}{1+n}\right]^{1/\beta} \qquad (7)$$

Over and above that we shall compare the relative magnitudes of k' and k". The evaluation of (2) and (7) furnishes a critical level of the future consumption elasticity:

$$\delta' = \frac{(1+n)(1-t)\alpha - (t-g)n}{(1-t)\beta n} \qquad (8)$$

First, if $\delta < \delta'$, then $k' > k''$. That is to say, under a high rate of time preference, the dd line will not cut across the kk line. For that reason, there will not be a steady state. The other way round, if $\delta > \delta'$, then $k' < k''$. Under a low rate of time preference, there can possibly be a point of intersection and, thus, a steady state. In the numerical example with $\alpha = 0.2$, $g = 0.2$, $t = 0.19$ and $n = 1.427$, the critical level is $\delta' = 0.44$.

The phase diagram in figure 4.2 rests on the assumption that a long-run equilibrium does in fact exist. The necessary and sufficient condition for the existence of a long-run equilibrium has already been established in the foregoing section. The lesson taught by the phase diagram is that there are two long-run equilibria $k_1 > k_2$, the first being stable, the second unstable. The shock and policy dynamics is isomorphic to that experienced in the Solow model.

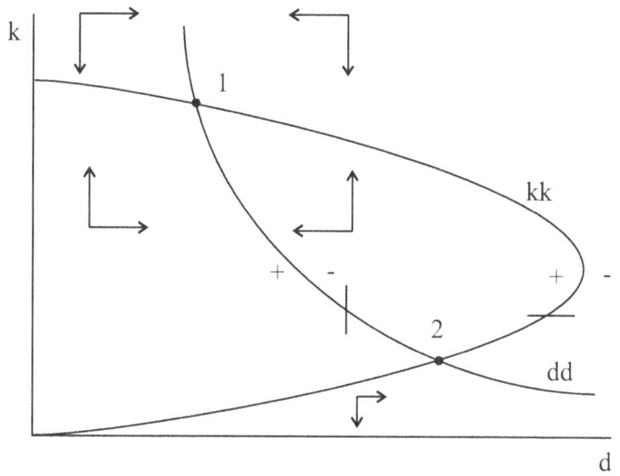

Figure 4.2
Fixed Tax Rate
(Overlapping Generations)

4.2.4 Summary

As a rule, no steady state does exist. Starting from a balanced budget, a reduction of the tax rate increases the deficit ratio, thereby displacing investment per head. In the long run, public debt per head tends to explode, hence capital per head shrinks back to zero. As an exception, if the future consumption elasticity is very high and if the primary deficit ratio is extremely low, two distinct steady states do exist, a stable one and an unstable one. As a consequence, a fixed tax rate generally cannot be sustained. This is in remarkable opposition to a fixed deficit ratio, that clearly can be sustained. Luckily, the government can switch from one regime to another.

4.3 Fixing the Deficit Per Head

4.3.1 The Short-Run Equilibrium

The first point refers to the dynamics of public debt. The government spends a certain amount per head of the active workers on goods and services $G = gN$ with $g = const$. In addition the government borrows a given sum per head of the active workers $B = bN$ with $b = const$. Public debt and the budget deficit of the current period add up to public debt of the subsequent period $D_{+1} = D + B$. Moreover the government levies a lumpsum tax per head of the active workers $T = tN$ with $t = const$. The government disburses the interest rate r on public debt D, so public interest equals rD. The government budget constraint is $B + T = G + rD$. Paying heed to the behavioural functions, the identity can be expressed as $bN + tN = gN + rD$. Here the government fixes purchases per head and the deficit per head, while it accommodates the lumpsum tax.

The second point refers to capital dynamics. Suppose that the lumpsum tax is paid by the young. Therefore the net wage rate of the representative worker is $w - t$. The net wage rate, diminished by consumption per head, provides savings per head, in the working period respectively $s = w - t - c^1$. Savings per head bear the interest rate r, hence consumption per head in the retirement period is $c^2 = (w - t - c^1)(1 + r)$. On these grounds, the individual budget constraint can be written as $c^1 + c^2/(1 + r) = w - t$. The representative worker maximizes utility subject to his budget constraint. Accordingly, consumption per head of the young is $c^1 = \gamma(w - t)$, and savings per head of the young are $s = \delta(w - t)$. Savings per head, multiplied by the number of active workers, yield savings of the young $S = sN$. From this one can deduce $S = \beta\delta Y - \delta tN$. Savings of the young this period confine the total of public debt and private capital next period $D_{+1} + K_{+1} = S$.

On this basis, the short-run equilibrium can be enshrined in a system of six equations:

$$Y = K^{\alpha}N^{\beta} \tag{1}$$

$$r = \alpha Y / K \tag{2}$$

$$D_{+1} + K_{+1} = \beta\delta Y - \delta tN \tag{3}$$

$$D_{+1} = D + bN \tag{4}$$

$$bN + tN = gN + rD \tag{5}$$

$$N_{+1} = (1+n)N \tag{6}$$

Here r, t, D_{+1}, K_{+1}, N_{+1} and Y are endogenous.

In per capita terms, the temporary equilibrium looks like this:

$$y = k^{\alpha} \tag{7}$$

$$r = \alpha y / k \tag{8}$$

$$(1+n)d_{+1} + (1+n)k_{+1} = \beta\delta y - \delta t \tag{9}$$

$$(1+n)d_{+1} = d + b \tag{10}$$

$$b + t = g + rd \tag{11}$$

Correspondingly, d_{+1}, k_{+1}, r, t and y adapt themselves.

4.3.2 The Long-Run Equilibrium

In the long-run equilibrium, public debt per head and capital per head come to a halt $d_{+1} = d$ and $k_{+1} = k$. That is why the permanent equilibrium takes the following shape:

$$y = k^{\alpha} \tag{1}$$

$$r = \alpha y / k \tag{2}$$

$$(1+n)d + (1+n)k = \beta\delta y - \delta t \tag{3}$$

$$nd = b \tag{4}$$

$$b + t = g + rd \tag{5}$$

Here d, k, r, t and y are endogenous.

Beyond that we shall probe into the relationship between the deficit per head and capital per head. Solve (5) for t, noting $d = b/n$ and $r = \alpha k^{-\beta}$ to reach $t = g + \alpha b k^{-\beta}/n - b$. Then put this into (3), calling attention to $y = k^{\alpha}$ and $d = b/n$, to arrive at:

$$b = \frac{\beta\delta k^{\alpha} - (1+n)k - \delta g}{(1+n)/n + \alpha\delta k^{-\beta}/n - \delta} \tag{6}$$

Thanks to (6), figure 4.3 plots capital per head as a function of the deficit per head. Obviously there exists, a critical deficit per head b', thus three cases emerge. First, if b < b', there will be two long-run equilibria. Second if b = b', there will be a unique long-run equilibrium. And third, if b > b', there will be no long-run equilibirium whatsoever.

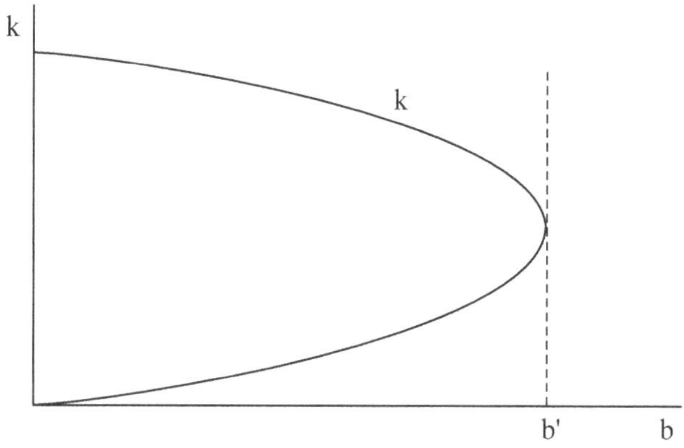

Figure 4.3
Deficit Per Head and Capital Per Head
(Overlapping Generations)

4.3.3 The Optimal Deficit Per Head

Also we shall inquire into the deficit per head that maximizes consumption per head. Simultaneously this deficit per head maximizes utility, since there is no distortionary tax. Insert the golden rule r = n into the government budget constraint b + t = g + rd and take account of nd = b to gain t = g. Phrased differently, the tax per head matches government purchases per head. Then substitute $y = k^{\alpha}$, d = b/n and t = g into (3) from section 4.3.2 to achieve b/n + b + (1 + n)k = $\beta\delta k^{\alpha} - \delta g$. Finally eliminate k by making use of r = n, $r = \alpha k^{-\beta}$ as well as $k = (\alpha / n)^{1/\beta}$ and regroup:

$$b^* = \frac{\beta\delta(\alpha / n)^{\alpha/\beta} - (1+n)(\alpha / n)^{1/\beta} - \delta g}{1/n+1} \qquad (1)$$

This is the optimum deficit per head.

Table 4.3 makes clear the influence of the saving ratio on the optimal deficit per head, resting on the parameter values α = 0.2, g = 0.2 and n = 1.427. Regard for instance γ = 0.5, which means no discount of future consumption. In this environment, the optimum deficit per head amounts to – 0.04. Put another way, the government should lend money, to the private sector in order to stimulate capital formation. Incidentally, the optimum deficit ratio is – 0.06. And a rise in the saving ratio occasions a fall in the optimum deficit per head.

Table 4.3: Saving Ratio and Optimal Deficit Per Head

γ	b^*	b^*/y
0.5	- 0.04	- 0.06
0.6	- 0.05	- 0.09
0.7	- 0.07	- 0.12

4.3.4 Stability and a Shock

The temporary equilibrium can be viewed as a system of two difference equations $d_{+1} = p(d, k)$ and $k_{+1} = q(d, k)$. It is well known from section 4.3.1 that

$$(1 + n)d_{+1} = d + b \tag{1}$$

This furnishes $\partial d_{+1}/\partial d = 1/(1 + n) < 1$. Then set $d_{+1} = d$:

$$d = b/n \tag{2}$$

Due to (2) figure 4.4 exhibits the vertical dd line.

Over and above that address k_{+1}. Put (7) and (10) into (9) from section 4.3.1, respectively, to accomplish $(1 + n)k_{+1} = \beta\delta k^{\alpha} - \delta t - d - b$. Further get rid of t with the help of $b + t = g + rd$, $r = \alpha k^{-\beta}$ and $t = g + \alpha d k^{-\beta} - b$:

$$(1+n)k_{+1} = \beta\delta k^{\alpha} - \delta(g + \alpha d k^{-\beta} - b) - d - b \tag{3}$$

An expansion of d brings about a contraction of k_{+1}. Moreover set $k_{+1} = k$ and reshuffle terms:

$$d = \frac{\beta\delta k^{\alpha} - (1+n)k - \delta g - \gamma b}{1 + \alpha\delta k^{-\beta}} \tag{4}$$

Figure 4.4 reveals the backward bending kk line, too. As a finding, the phase diagram contains two permanent equilibria, one of them being stable, the other unstable.

For the remainder of this section we shall throw some light on the process of adjustment induced by a permanent increase in the deficit per head, granted $b < b'$. In this situation, there are two long-run equilibria, a stable one and an unstable one. Choose the stable case. Initially the economy is in the long-run equilibrium. The budget deficit and public public debt, in per capita terms respectively, do not move. Investment per head and capital per head are uniform. Output, income and

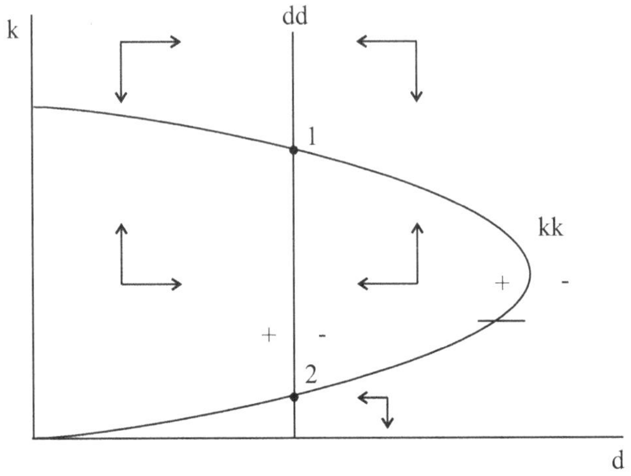

Figure 4.4
Fixed Deficit Per Head
(Overlapping Generations)

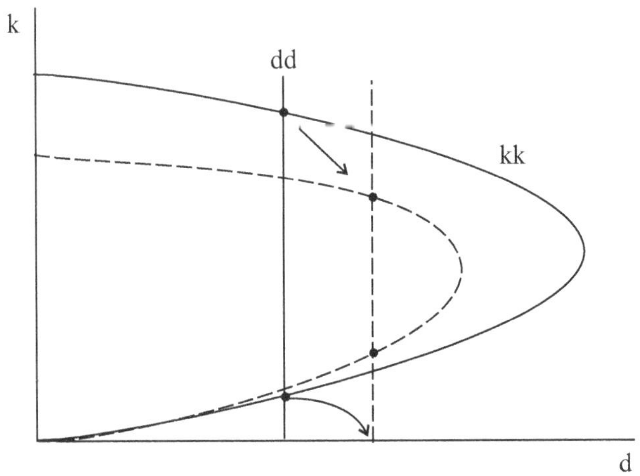

Figure 4.5
Increase in Deficit Per Head

consumption per head hold fast. Against this background, the government raises the deficit per head. In the phase diagram, the dd line shifts to the right, whereas the kk line shifts to the left. The streamline marks how the economy develops over time, cf. figure 4.5.

In the short run, this measure supplants investment per head. Owing to the budget constraint, the government is in a position to lower the lumpsum tax, thereby improving consumption per head. In the intermediate run, public debt per head piles up, while capital per head becomes dismantled. The decrease of capital brings about a decrease of output, income and consumption, in per capita terms. As the interest rate and public debt per head go up, so does public interest per head. To serve this, the government must lift the lumpsum tax. With the lapse of time, the economy drifts towards a new long-run equilibrium. The budget deficit and public debt, in per capita terms, do not move any more. Investment per head and capital per head are again invariant. Properly speaking, public debt per head attains a higher level, whereas capital per head settles down at a lower level.

4.3.5 Summary

The investigation demonstrates the existence of a critical deficit per head. As long as the deficit per head falls short of the critical level, there will be two long-run equilibria, a stable one and an unstable one. But as soon as the deficit per head exceeds the critical level, there will be no long-run equilibrium at all. With a low deficit per head, an increase in the deficit per head reduces capital per head. On the other hand, with a high deficit per head, an increase in the deficit per head drives capital per head down to zero abruptly. In addition, there exists an optimal deficit per head that maximizes consumption per head. If the saving ratio is large, the optimal deficit per head will be positive. Conversely, if the saving ratio is small, the optimal deficit per head will be negative. Empirical evidence seems to suggest that the government should make loans to the private sector. To put it in one sentence, a fixed deficit per head generally can be sustained.

4.4 Fixing the Tax Per Head

4.4.1 The Short-Run Equilibrium and the Long-Run Equilibrium

First catch a glimpse of budget dynamics. The government buys a specified volume of goods and services per head $G = gN$ with $g = const.$ Moreover the government imposes a lumpsum tax $T = tN$ with $t = const.$ The excess of public expenditures over tax revenue makes up the budget deficit $B = G + rD - T$. Public debt and the budget deficit this period add up to public debt next period $D_{+1} = D + B$. From this one can infer $D_{+1} = D + gN + rD - tN$.

In full analogy to the preceding sections, the short-run equilibrium can be represented by a system of five equations:

$$Y = K^{\alpha} N^{\beta} \tag{1}$$

$$r = \alpha Y / K \tag{2}$$

$$D_{+1} + K_{+1} = \beta\delta Y - \delta t N \tag{3}$$

$$D_{+1} = D + gN + rD - tN \tag{4}$$

$$N_{+1} = (1 + n)N \tag{5}$$

Here r, D_{+1}, K_{+1}, N_{+1} and Y are endogenous. Now it is useful to do the analysis in per capita terms:

$$y = k^{\alpha} \tag{6}$$

$$r = \alpha y / k \tag{7}$$

$$(1+n)d_{+1} + (1+n)k_{+1} = \beta\delta y - \delta t \tag{8}$$

$$(1+n)d_{+1} = d + g + rd - t \tag{9}$$

In this version d_{+1}, k_{+1}, r and y adjust themselves.

In the steady state, public debt per head and capital per head stop to adjust $d_{+1} = d$ and $k_{+1} = k$. For that reason, the long-run equilibrium can be described by a system of four equations:

$$y = k^{\alpha} \tag{10}$$

$$r = \alpha y / k \tag{11}$$

$$(1+n)d + (1+n)k = \beta\delta y - \delta t \tag{12}$$

$$nd = g + rd - t \tag{13}$$

Here d, k, r and y are endogenous.

4.4.2 Stability

We start right out with equation (9) from section 4.4.1:

$$(1+n)d_{+1} = d + g + rd - t \tag{1}$$

This gives $\partial d_{+1}/\partial d = (1 + r)/(1 + n)$. Because of that, two cases are to be distinguished. If $r \lesseqgtr n$, then $\partial d_{+1}/\partial d \lesseqgtr 1$. Further install $r = \alpha k^{-\beta}$ in (1):

$$(1+n)d_{+1} = d + g + \alpha d k^{-\beta} - t \tag{2}$$

From this follows a critical value of capital per head $k' = (\alpha / n)^{1/\beta}$. If $k \lesseqgtr k'$, then $\partial d_{+1}/\partial d \gtreqless 1$.

Now set $d_{+1} = d$ in (1) and rearrange:

$$d = \frac{g - t}{n - r} \tag{3}$$

Let $t < g$. In this condition two cases can occur. As long as the interest rate stays below the natural rate, public debt per head will be positive. However, as soon as the interest rate surpasses the natural rate, public debt per head will be negative. This is a contradiction in terms, so one may expect that there will be no long-run equilibrium. Henceforth we postulate that the interest rate is less than the natural rate, thus public debt per head will be positive. What is more, as the interest rate converges to the natural rate from below, public debt per head tends to infinity. Besides take account of $r = \alpha k^{-\beta}$ in (3):

$$d = \frac{g - t}{n - \alpha k^{-\beta}} \tag{4}$$

d descends when k mounts. And d goes to $(g - t)/n$, when k becomes very large. Accordingly figure 4.6 portrays the downward sloping dd line.

Next we tackle k_{+1}. Dispense with d_{+1} and y in (8) by virtue of (9) and (6) from section 4.4.1, respectively:

$$(1 + n)k_{+1} = \beta\delta k^{\alpha} + \gamma t - d - g - rd \tag{5}$$

This spins off $\partial k_{+1} / \partial d = -(1 + r)/(1 + n) < 0$. At last set $k_{+1} = k$ and note $r = \alpha k^{-\beta}$:

$$d = \frac{\beta\delta k^{\alpha} - (1 + n)k + \gamma t - g}{1 + \alpha k^{-\beta}} \tag{6}$$

On that grounds figure 4.6 depicts the backward bending kk line. The message conveyed by the phase diagram is that there are two long-run equilibria, one of them being stable, the other unstable.

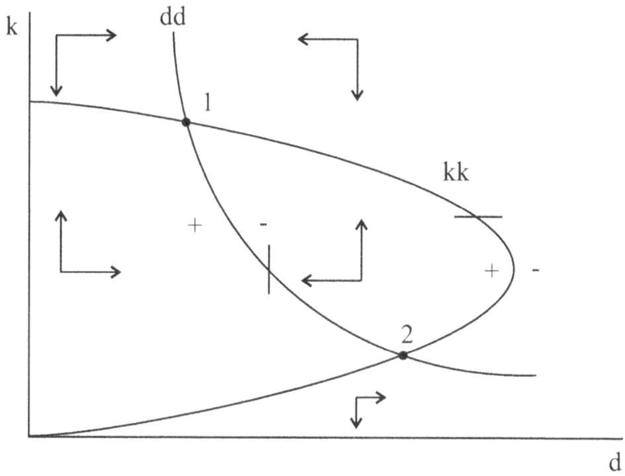

Figure 4.6
Fixed Tax Per Head
(Overlapping Generations)

4.4.3 Summary

Taking the same avenue as in section 4.2, the following conclusions can be reached. As a rule, there will be no steady state. Departing from a balanced budget, a reduction of the lumpsum tax increases the deficit per head, thereby displacing investment per head. In the long run, public debt per head proliferates without bounds, which squeezes capital per head down to zero. As an exception, if the future consumption elasticity is very high and if the primary deficit per head is extremely low, there will be two steady states, a stable one and an unstable one. As an outcome, a fixed tax per head generally cannot be sustained.

5 Infinite Horizon

5.1 Fixing the Deficit Ratio

5.1.1 The Short-Run Equilibrium

In the current chapter, we shall consider a third hypothesis with respect to saving behaviour. In the Solow model, we assumed a fixed saving ratio. In the overlapping generations model, we assumed intertemporal optimization within a finite horizon. Now, in place of that, we shall assume intertemporal optimization within an inifinite horizon. The basic idea is due to Ramsey (1928). To begin with, in section 5.1, the government fixes the deficit ratio. Then, in section 5.2, the government fixes the tax rate. And finally, in section 5.3, the government optimizes the deficit ratio.

Firms produce a single commodity Y by means of capital K and labour N. For the sake of simplicity let technology be of the Cobb-Douglas type, exhibiting constant returns to scale $Y = K^{\alpha}N^{\beta}$ with $\alpha > 0$, $\beta > 0$ and $\alpha + \beta = 1$. Every worker has got a job. Output can be used for consumption and investment $Y = C + I$. The government does not provide goods and services, as opposed to the preceding sections. Investment in turn adds to the stock of capital $\dot{K} = I$. Let labour grow at the natural rate $\dot{N} = nN$ with n = const. It is helpful to reformulate this in per capita terms as $y = k^{\alpha}$ and $y = c + i$. Here c denotes consumption per head, and i is investment per head. Take the time derivative of capital per head $k = K/N$ to realize $\dot{k} = i - nk$. Owing to $i = y - c$ and $y = k^{\alpha}$, this can be written as $\dot{k} = k^{\alpha} - c - nk$.

Households maximize discounted utility within an infinite horizon:

$$W = \int_0^{\infty} e^{-\rho u} \log c \, du \tag{1}$$

subject to $\dot{k} = k^{\alpha} - c - nk$. Here log c stands for the utility function, ρ is the discount rate and u is time. The solution to this control problem is

$\dot{c} = (\alpha k^{-\beta} - n - \rho)c$, cf. Burmeister and Dobell (1970), Blanchard and Fischer (1989) as well as Chiang (1992). Of course, this line of argument rests on rather strong assumptions. Agents hold rational expectations, they have perfect foresight and optimize into an infinite future, even though they have only finite lives. To a certain extent this hypothesis can be justified by the dynastic motive of bequests, cf. Barro (1974).

Firms maximize profits under perfect competition, so the interest rate corresponds to the marginal product of capital $r = \alpha Y/K$. Likewise the wage rate harmonizes with the marginal product of labour $w = \beta Y/N$. Next we talk about the dynamics of public debt. The government makes transfers to the private sector. More precisely, the government hands over a specific fraction of national income $G = gY$ with $g = \text{const}$. In addition, the government borrows a fixed share of national income $B = bY$ with $b = \text{const}$. The budget deficit in turn augments public debt $\dot{D} = B$. From this one can deduce $\dot{d} = by - nd$. The government pays the interest rate r on public debt D, hence public interest amounts to rD. Moreover the government collects a tax at the flat rate t on both factor income and debt income $T = t(Y + rD)$. The government budget constraint is $B + T = G + rD$. After inserting the behavioural functions, it can be restated in per capita terms $by + t(y + rd) = gy + rd$. Here the government presets the transfer ratio and the deficit ratio, while it adjusts the tax rate appropriately.

Further have a look at capital dynamics. Factor income plus transfers received plus public interest minus tax load make up disposable income $Y_d = Y + G + rD - T$. Combine this with $B + T = G + rD$ and $B = bY$ to attain $Y_d = (1+b)Y$. Households save a certain proportion of disposable income $S = sY_d$ with s = "const", which implies $S = s(1 + b)Y$. Disposable income can either be consumed or saved $Y_d = C + S$. From this one can infer $C = (1 - s)(1 + b)Y$ and $c = (1 - s)(1 + b)y$.

Having laid this foundation, the short-run equilibrium can be captured by a system of seven equations:

$$y = k^{\alpha} \tag{2}$$

$$r = \alpha y / k \tag{3}$$

$$\dot{k} = y - c - nk \tag{4}$$

$$\dot{c} = (r - n - \rho)c \tag{5}$$

$$c = (1 - s)(1 + b)y \tag{6}$$

$$\dot{d} = by - nd \tag{7}$$

$$by + t(y + rd) = gy + rd \tag{8}$$

In this version α, ρ, b, c, d, g, k and n are exogenous, where $\dot{c}$, $\dot{d}$, $\dot{k}$, r, s, t and y are endogenous.

5.1.2 The Long-Run Equilibrium

In the steady state, consumption per head, public debt per head and capital per head come to a standstill $\dot{c} = \dot{d} = \dot{k} = 0$. Accordingly the long-run equilibrium can be enshrined in a system of seven equations:

$$y = k^{\alpha} \tag{1}$$

$$r = \alpha y / k \tag{2}$$

$$y = c + nk \tag{3}$$

$$r = n + \rho \tag{4}$$

$$c = (1 - s)(1 + b)y \tag{5}$$

$$nd = by \tag{6}$$

$$by + t(y + rd) = gy + rd \tag{7}$$

In this condition c, d, k, r, s, t and y are endogenous.

Beyond that we shall solve the system (1) to (7) for the endogenous variables. (1) together with (2) and (4) provides:

$$k^{\beta} = \frac{\alpha}{n+\rho} \tag{8}$$

An increase in the deficit ratio leaves no impact on capital per head. An increase in the natural rate reduces capital per head, and the same applies to an increase in the discount rate.

Over and above that we shall determine the optimal saving ratio. Eliminate c in (3) with the help of (5) to accomplish s = (by + nk)/(1 + b)y. Then pay heed to (1), observing (8):

$$s^{*} = \frac{\alpha n + (n+\rho)b}{(n+\rho)(1+b)} \tag{9}$$

A rise in the deficit ratio pushes up the optimal saving ratio s^{*}. The same is true of a rise in the natural rate. On the other hand, a rise in the discount rate pulls down the optimal saving ratio. To illustrate this, take a numerical example with $\alpha = 0.2$ and n = 0.03. Table 5.1 demonstrates the way in which the optimal saving ratio hinges on the deficit ratio and the discount rate.

Besides get rid of y in (6) by making use of (1) and (8):

$$d = \frac{b}{n}\left(\frac{\alpha}{n+\rho}\right)^{\alpha/\beta} \tag{10}$$

A lift in the deficit ratio enhances public debt per head. A lift in the natural rate, however, depresses public debt per head. And a lift in the discount rate works in the same direction.

Last but not least, substitute d = by/n as well as $r = n + \rho$ into (7) and regroup:

$$t = \frac{gn + b\rho}{n + bn + b\rho} \tag{11}$$

Here a critical discount rate emerges $\rho' = gn/(1-g)$. If $\rho \lesseqgtr \rho'$, then $dt/db \lesseqgtr 0$. Under a low discount rate, an increase in the deficit ratio cuts back the tax rate.

Conversely, under a high discount rate, an increase in the deficit ratio brings up the tax rate. In a numerical example with g = 0.2 and n = 0.03, the critical level is $\rho' = 0.01$. Henceforth let the discount rate surpass the critical level, thus an increase in the deficit ratio boosts the tax rate.

Table 5.1
Optimal Saving Ratio

	ρ			
b	0	0.01	0.02	0.03
0	0.20	0.15	0.12	0.10
0.01	0.21	0.16	0.13	0.11
0.02	0.22	0.17	0.14	0.12

5.1.3 Stability

The short-run equilibrium can be interpreted as a system of two differential equations:

$$\dot{k} = p(k,s) \tag{1}$$

$$\dot{s} = q(k,s) \tag{2}$$

(4) in conjunction with (6) and (2) from section 5.1.1, respectively, supply:

$$\dot{k} = (s + bs - b)k^{\alpha} - nk \tag{3}$$

Apparently an increase in s raises $\dot{k}$. Then set $\dot{k} = 0$ to achieve:

$$s = \frac{nk^{\beta} + b}{1 + b} \tag{4}$$

For k = 0 it is valid that s = b/(1 + b). Correspondingly figure 5.1 plots the upward sloping $\dot{k} = 0$ line.

Next come to grips with $\dot{s}$ = q(k, s). Put (3) and (6) into (5) from section 5.1.1, respectively:

$$\dot{c} = (\alpha k^{-\beta} - n - \rho)(1 - s)(1 + b)y \tag{5}$$

Moreover take the time derivative of (6) from section 5.1.1:

$$\dot{c} = (1 + b)\left[(1 - s)\dot{y} - \dot{s}y\right] \tag{6}$$

Now equate (5) and (6), then solve for $\dot{s}$:

$$\dot{s} = (1 - s)\dot{y} / y - (\alpha k^{-\beta} - n - \rho)(1 - s) \tag{7}$$

In addition express $y = k^{\alpha}$ in terms of growth rates $\dot{y} / y = \alpha \dot{k} / k$ and note (3):

$$\dot{y} / y = (s + bs - b)\alpha k^{-\beta} - \alpha n \tag{8}$$

Finally dispense with $\dot{y} / y$ in (7) thanks to (8):

$$\dot{s} = (1 - s)(\beta n + \rho) - (1 - s)^2 (1 + b)\alpha k^{-\beta} \tag{9}$$

As k climbs, so does $\dot{s}$. Further set $\dot{s} = 0$ and reshuffle:

$$s = 1 - \frac{(\beta n + \rho)k^{\beta}}{(1 + b)\alpha} \tag{10}$$

For k = 0 it holds s = 1. As a finding, figure 5.1 graphs the downward sloping $\dot{s} = 0$ line.

Assembling all component parts, figure 5.1 presents the phase diagram. Obviously the long-run equilibrium is a saddle point, so it will be stable. Beyond that, figure 5.2 depicts the saddle path. Incidentally, (7) and (2) from section 5.1.1, respectively, yield:

$$\dot{d} = bk^{\alpha} - nd \tag{11}$$

Public debt per head will be stable, too, since $\partial \dot{d} / \partial d = -n < 0$.

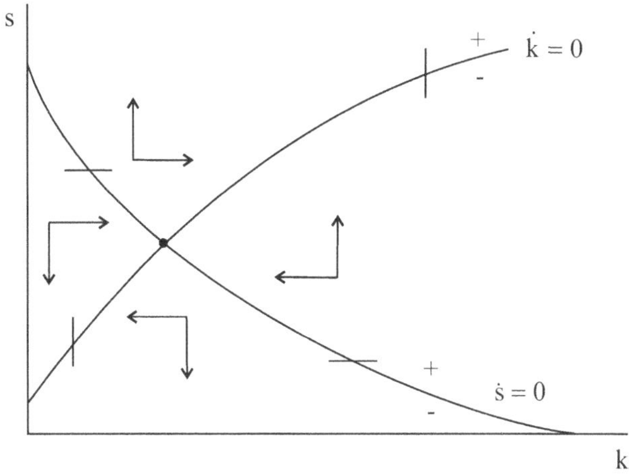

Figure 5.1
Fixed Deficit Ratio
(Infinite Horizon)

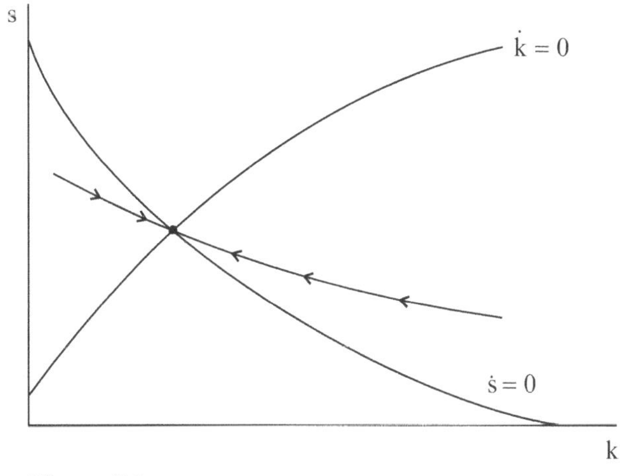

Figure 5.2
Saddle Path

5.1.4 Some Shocks

First regard an increase in the deficit ratio. At the beginning, the economy rests in the long-run equilibrium. The budget deficit and public debt, in per capita terms respectively, do not move. Investment per head and capital per head are uniform. Output, income and consumption per head do not change. Against this background, the government lifts the deficit ratio. As an instantaneous response, households lift the saving ratio so as to keep investment per head constant. By virtue of the budget constraint, the government is able to reduce the tax rate in such a way that consumption per head remains unaffected on balance. In the phase diagram, the $\dot{k} = 0$ line shifts to the left, whereas the $\dot{s} = 0$ line shifts upwards, cf. figure 5.3. Strictly speaking, the economy makes a jump from the old long-run equilibrium into the new one.

In the medium run, the rise in the deficit ratio leads to the accumulation of public debt per head. Contrary to that, the process has no influence on investment per head, capital per head and output per head. The piling up of public debt compels the government to disburse more interest, in per capita terms respectively. Therefore, owing to the budget constraint, the government must enhance the tax rate. Over time the economy tends to a new long-run equilibrium. The budget deficit and public debt, in per capita terms, cease to move. Investment per head and capital per head are still uniform. More exactly, public debt per head reaches a higher level, while capital per head stays at the original level. Figures 5.4 to 5.7 elucidate the time paths of the chief variables. The policy measure has no real effects, as can be seen from figure 5.6. Of course the whole story reminds one of Ricardian equivalenve, cf. Barro (1974).

Second contemplate an increase in the natural rate of labour growth. Initially the economy reproduces itself in the steady state. Public debt per head and capital per head do not vary. Then surprisingly the natural rate springs up. As an immediate reaction, households lower the saving ratio. In the phase diagram, the $\dot{k} = 0$ line is transposed to the left, whereas the $\dot{s} = 0$ line is transposed downwards, cf. figure 5.8. In the short term, consumption per head goes up, while investment per head comes down. In the intermediate term, capital per head declines, which depresses output and income per head. That is why the

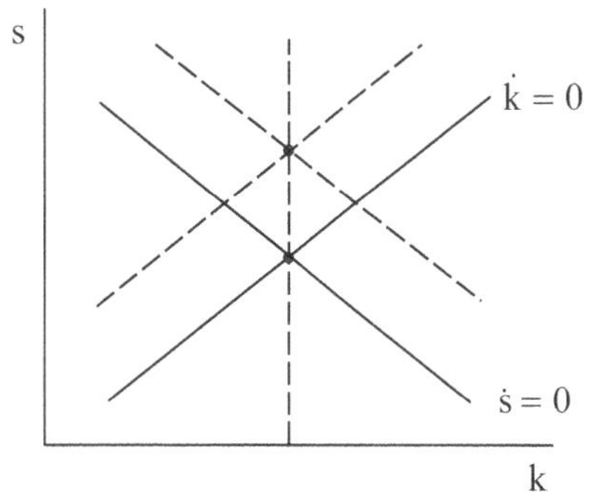

Figure 5.3
Increase in Deficit Ratio

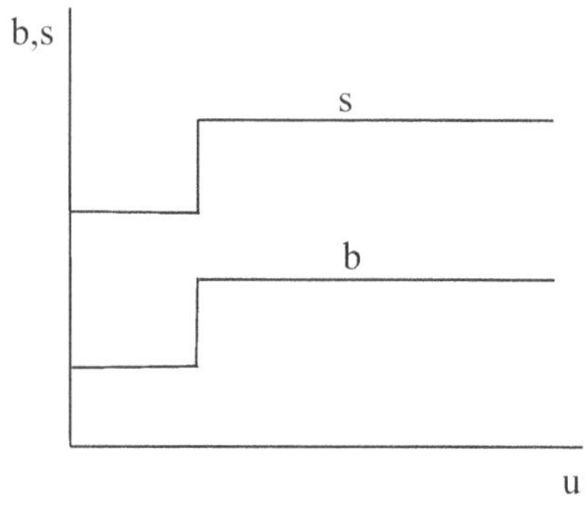

Figure 5.4
Optimal Saving Ratio

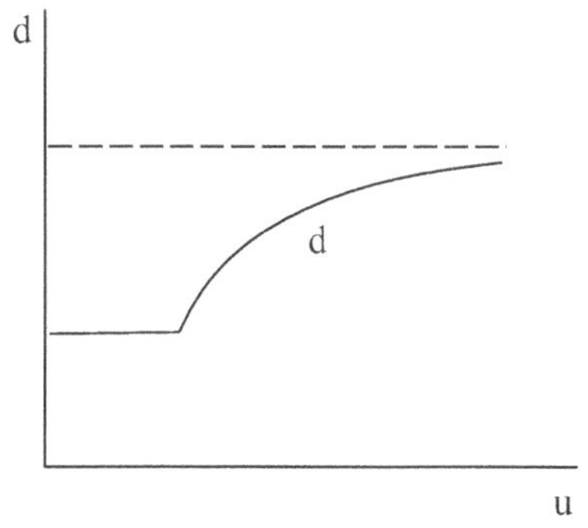

Figure 5.5
Public Debt Per Head

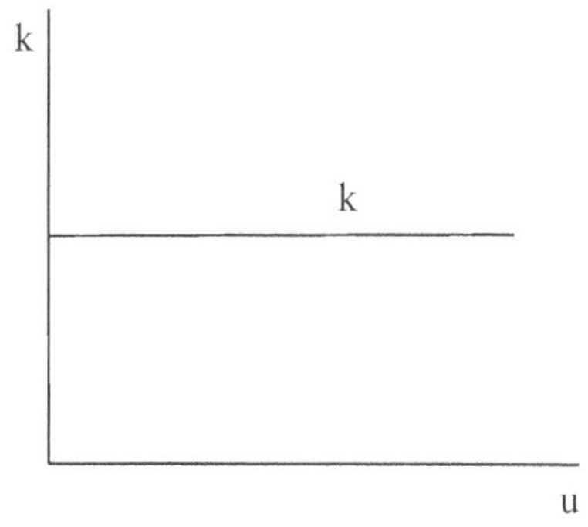

Figure 5.6
Capital Per Head

deficit per head and public debt per head begin to fall. In the long term, the economy converges to a new steady state. Public debt per head and capital per head do no longer vary. Figures 5.9 and 5.10 map the trajectories of some relevant variables.

Third we address an increase in the discount rate. At the start, the economy is in a stationary equilibrium. Public debt per head and capital per head are constant. Then suddenly the discount rate rises. At once households cut the saving ratio. In the phase diagram, the $\dot{s} = 0$ line glides downwards, cf. figure 5.11. In the short run, the shock expands consumption per head and contracts investment per head. In the medium run, capital per head decreases, thereby curtailing income per head. For that reason, the deficit per head and public debt per head dwindle, too. In due course, the economy gravitates to a new stationary equilibrium. At last public debt per head and capital per head settle down. Figures 5.12 and 5.13 illuminate the associated time paths.

5.1.5 Summary

The long-run equilibrium is a saddle point that proves to be stable. Suppose for instance that the government increases the deficit ratio. Instantaneously, to counteract this, households increase the saving ratio. Thus the government action leaves no impact on capital per head. It has no real effects, neither in the short run nor in the long run. As a consequence, a fixed deficit ratio always can be sustained.

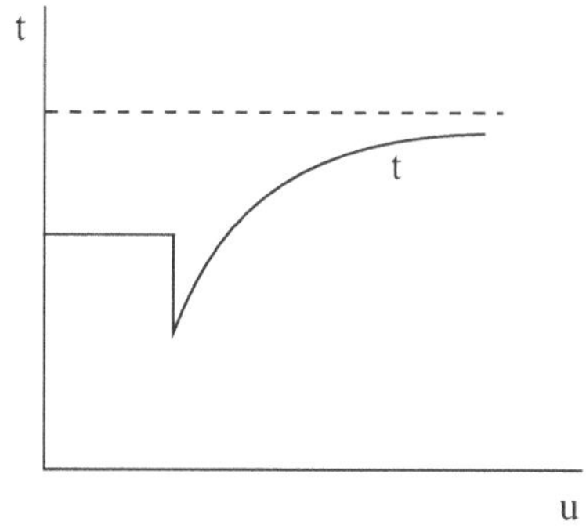

Figure 5.7
Tax Rate

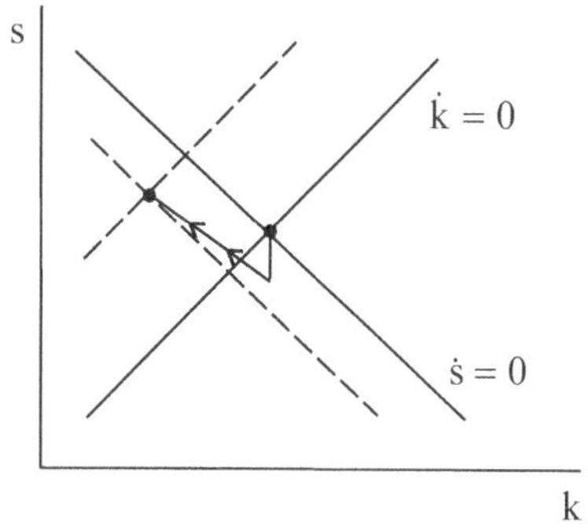

Figure 5.8
Increase in Labour Growth

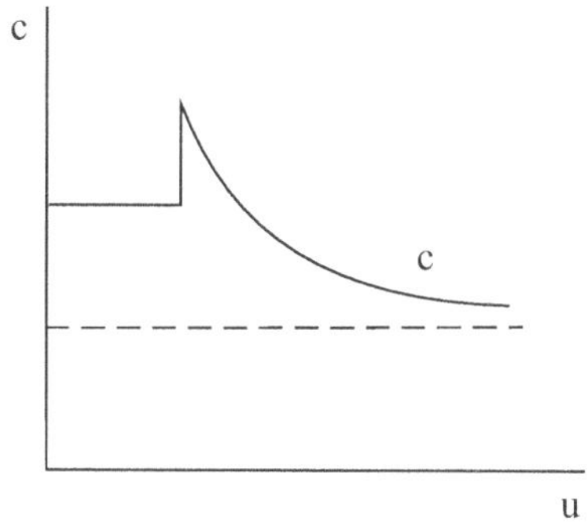

Figure 5.9
Consumption Per Head

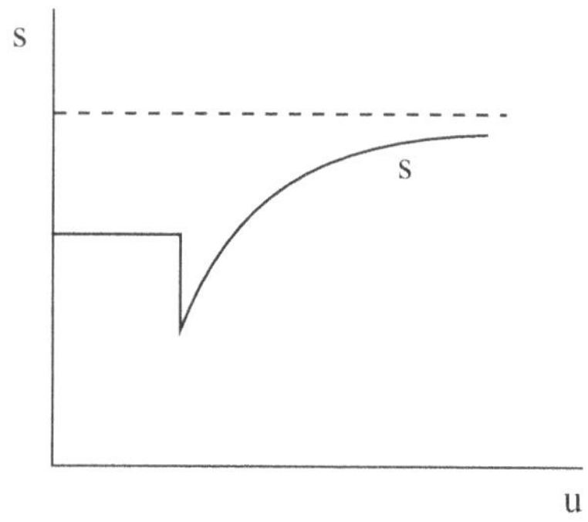

Figure 5.10
Optimal Saving Ratio

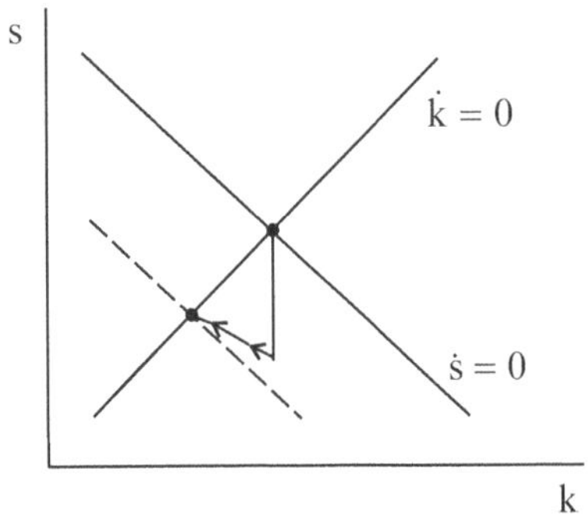

Figure 5.11
Increase in Discount Rate

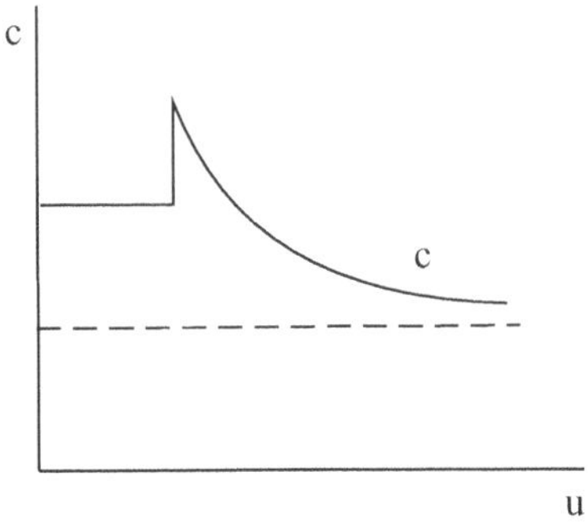

Figure 5.12
Consumption Per Head

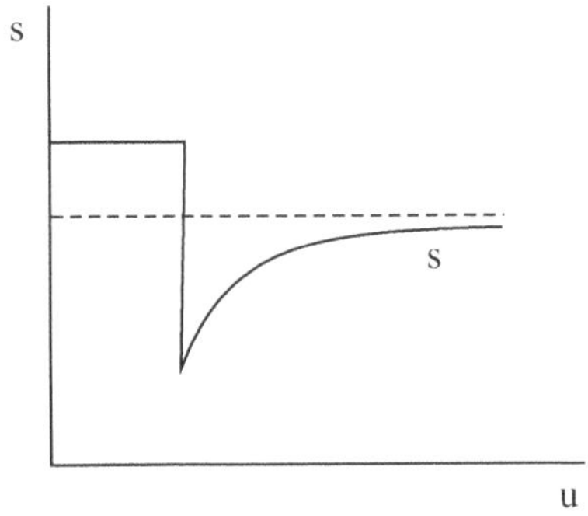

Figure 5.13
Optimal Saving Ratio

5.2 Fixing the Tax Rate

5.2.1 The Short-Run Equilibrium

Equations (1) to (4) from section 5.1.1 are true in this context as well. Let us begin with budget dynamics. The government makes transfers to the private sector $G = gY$ with $g = \text{const}$. In addition the government levies a tax at the flat rate $t = \text{const}$ on both factor income and debt income $T = t(Y + rD)$. The budget deficit states the difference between public expenditures and tax earnings $B = G + rD - T$. The budget deficit in turn adds to public debt $\dot{D} = B$. From this one can infer $\dot{D} = gY + rD - t(Y + rD)$ and $\dot{d} = gy + rd - t(y + rd) - nd$.

The next point relates to investment dynamics. Disposable income comprises factor income, government transfers and public interest, net after tax respectively $Y_d = Y + G + rD - T$. Take account of $G = gY$ and $T = t(Y + rD)$ to verify $Y_d = (1 - t)(Y + rD) + gY$. Households put aside a certain fraction of disposable income for future consumption $S = sY_d$ with s = "const". In other words, disposable income serves for consumption and savings $Y_d = C + S$. This involves $C = (1 - s)(1 - t)(Y + rD) + (1 - s)gY$.

On these grounds, the short-run equilibrium can be caught by a system of six equations:

$$y = k^{\alpha} \tag{1}$$

$$r = \alpha y / k \tag{2}$$

$$\dot{k} = y - c - nk \tag{3}$$

$$\dot{c} = (r - n - \rho)c \tag{4}$$

$$c = (1 - s)(1 - t)(y + rd) + (1 - s)gy \tag{5}$$

$$\dot{d} = gy + rd - t(y + rd) - nd \tag{6}$$

Here α, ρ, c, d, g, k, n and t are exogenous, whereas $\dot{c}$, $\dot{d}$, $\dot{k}$, r, s and y are endogenous.

5.2.2 The Long-Run Equilibrium

In the steady state, consumption per head, public debt per head and capital per head are invariant $\dot{c} = \dot{d} = \dot{k} = 0$. Thus the long-run equilibrium can be laid out as follows:

$$y = k^{\alpha} \tag{1}$$

$$r = \alpha y / k \tag{2}$$

$$y = c + nk \tag{3}$$

$$r = n + \rho \tag{4}$$

$$c = (1-s)(1-t)(y + rd) + (1-s)gy \tag{5}$$

$$nd + t(y + rd) = gy + rd \tag{6}$$

In this condition c, d, k, r, s and y are endogenous.

Capital per head is the same size as under a fixed deficit ratio:

$$k^{\beta} = \frac{\alpha}{n+\rho} \tag{7}$$

Further substitute (4) into (6) and rearrange:

$$d = \frac{gy - ty}{n - (1-t)(n+\rho)} \tag{8}$$

Posit $t < g$. Then the assessment of (8) gives rise to a critical discount rate:

$$\rho' = \frac{nt}{1-t} \tag{9}$$

As long as the discount rate falls short of the critical value, public debt per head will be positive. In this situation, a long-run equilibrium does exist. But as soon as the discount rate exceeds the critical value, public debt per head will become negative. This seems to be somewhat like a paradox. Hence one may suspect that in this situation no long-run equilibrium does exist. In the numerical example with $n = 0.03$ and $t = 0.2$, the critical discount rate is very low $\rho' = 0.0075$.

5.2.3 A Tax Cut

Here we shall trace out the process generated by a permanent tax cut, provided $\rho > \rho'$. Accordingly no steady state does exist. Initially the economy reproduces itself in a steady state with $t = g$. The budget is balanced $b = 0$, so there is no public debt $d = 0$. Investment per head and capital per head are uniform. Under these circumstances, the government reduces the tax rate. As an instantaneous response, households increase the saving ratio. In the short run, the tax cut augments consumption per head. Owing to the budget constraint, the government must lift the deficit ratio, thereby diminishing investment per head, in spite of the increase in the saving ratio.

In the medium run, public debt per head builds up, while capital per head becomes dismantled. Due to the growth of public debt per head, the government has to pay more interest per head. To finance this, it must further lift the deficit ratio, which accelerates the growth of public debt per head. In the long run, public debt per head tends to explode. This in turn drives capital per head down to zero. Eventually the economy is bound to collapse.

5.2.4 Summary

As a rule, there will be no long-run equilibrium. As an exception, if the discount rate is very low, there will in fact be a long-run equilibrium. That is to say, a fixed tax rate generally cannot be sustained.

5.3 The Optimal Deficit Ratio

5.3.1 The Short-Run Equilibrium and the Long-Run Equilibrium

In sections 5.1 and 5.2, we started from the premise that private agents optimize within an infinite horizon. In the current section, instead, we postulate that it is the government who does the optimization. In full analogy to section 5.1, the short-run equilibrium can be encapsulated in a system of seven equations:

$$y = k^{\alpha} \tag{1}$$

$$r = \alpha y / k \tag{2}$$

$$\dot{k} = y - c - nk \tag{3}$$

$$\dot{c} = (r - n - \rho)c \tag{4}$$

$$c = (1 - s)(1 + b)y \tag{5}$$

$$\dot{d} = by - nd \tag{6}$$

$$by + t(y + rd) = gy + rd \tag{7}$$

Here α, ρ, c, d, g, k, n and s are exogenous, whereas b, $\dot{c}$, $\dot{d}$, $\dot{k}$, r, t and y are endogenous. As compared to section 5.1, the sole difference is that here the saving ratio is given, while the government optimizes the deficit ratio dynamically.

In the steady state, consumption per head, public debt per head and capital per head come to a halt $\dot{c} = \dot{d} = \dot{k} = 0$. Thus the long-run equilibrium can be written as follows:

$$y = k^{\alpha} \tag{8}$$

$$r = \alpha y / k \tag{9}$$

$$y = c + nk \tag{10}$$

$$r = n + \rho \tag{11}$$

$$c = (1 - s)(1 + b)y \tag{12}$$

$$nd = by \tag{13}$$

$$by + t(y + rd) = gy + rd \tag{14}$$

In this version b, c, d, k, r, t and y are endogenous.

Here a few comments are in place concerning the attributes of the steady state.

$$k^{\beta} = \frac{\alpha}{n + \rho} \tag{15}$$

holds in the same way as in the preceding sections. Now we shall derive the optimal deficit ratio. Combine (10) and (12), taking account of (8) and (15):

$$b^{*} = \frac{(n + \rho)s - \alpha n}{(n + \rho)(1 - s)} \tag{16}$$

An increase in the natural rate reduces the optimal deficit ratio. The other way round, an increase in the saving ratio elevates the optimal deficit ratio. And the same applies to an increase in the discount rate. More precisely, the analysis of (16) leads to a critical saving:

$$s' = \frac{\alpha n}{n + \rho} \tag{17}$$

If $s \gtrless s'$, then $b^{*} \gtrless 0$. Put another way, under a high saving ratio, the government should raise loans. Conversely, under a low saving ratio, the government should extend credit.

Next consider a numerical example, specifying $\alpha = 0.2$, $n = 0.03$ and $s = 0.1$. Table 5.2 shows the optimal deficit ratio as a function of the discount rate. When the government does not discount future consumption at all, the optimal deficit ratio is $- 0.11$. In this case, the government should lend money to the private sector in order to encourage capital formation. However, when the discount rate amounts to 0.04, the optimal deficit ratio is + 0.02. In this case, the government should borrow in order to check capital formation.

Incidentally, for $\rho = 0$, the optimal deficit ratio is $b^* = (s - \alpha)/(1 - s)$. This is equivalent to the results obtained in a Solow model with public transfers. Coming to an end, solve (13) for d and pay attention to (16), (8) as well as (15):

$$d = \frac{(n+\rho)s - \alpha n}{(n+\rho)(1-s)n}\left(\frac{\alpha}{n+\rho}\right)^{\alpha/\beta} \tag{18}$$

A lift in the saving ratio brings up public debt per head, and so on.

Table 5.2
Optimal Deficit Ratio

ρ	b^*
0	- 0.11
0.01	- 0.06
0.02	- 0.02
0.03	0
0.04	+ 0.02

5.3.2 Stability

The short-run equilibrium can be compressed to a system of two differential equations:

$$\dot{k} = p(k, b) \tag{1}$$

$$\dot{b} = q(k, b) \tag{2}$$

First get rid of y and c in (3) by making use of (1) and (5) from section 5.3.1, respectively:

$$\dot{k} = (s + bs - b)k^{\alpha} - nk \tag{3}$$

$\dot{k}$ drops as b climbs. Then set $\dot{k} = 0$ and regroup:

$$b = \frac{s - nk^{\beta}}{1 - s} \tag{4}$$

For k = 0, (4) simplifies to b = s/(1 – s). Correspondingly figure 5.14 portrays the negatively inclined $\dot{k} = 0$ line.

Second we shall probe into $\dot{b} = q(k, b)$. Insert (5) into (4) from section 5.3.1, respectively:

$$\dot{c} = (\alpha k^{-\beta} - n - \rho)(1 - s)(1 + b)y \tag{5}$$

Moreover take the time derivative of (5) from section 5.3.1:

$$\dot{c} = (1 - s)(\dot{y} + \dot{b}y + b\dot{y}) \tag{6}$$

Further equate (5) and (6), then solve for:

$$\dot{b} = (\alpha k^{-\beta} - n - \rho)(1 + b) - (1 + b)\dot{y} / y \tag{7}$$

Express $y = k^{\alpha}$ in terms of growth rates, observing (3):

$$\dot{y} / y = (s + bs - b)\alpha k^{-\beta} - \alpha n \tag{8}$$

Dispense with $\dot{y}/y$ in (7) thanks to (8):

$$\dot{b} = (1 + b)^2 (1 - s)\alpha k^{-\beta} - (1 + b)(\beta n + \rho) \tag{9}$$

$\dot{b}$ descends as k mounts. Finally set $\dot{b} = 0$ and reshuffle terms:

$$b = \frac{(\beta n + \rho)k^{\beta}}{(1 - s)\alpha} - 1 \tag{10}$$

For $k = 0$ it is valid that $b = -1$. As an outcome, figure 5.14 displays the positively inclined $\dot{b} = 0$ line.

Putting all pieces together, figure 5.14 offers the phase diagram. Evidently the long-run equilibrium is a saddle point that turns out to be stable. Over and above that, figure 5.15 visualizes the pertinent saddle path.

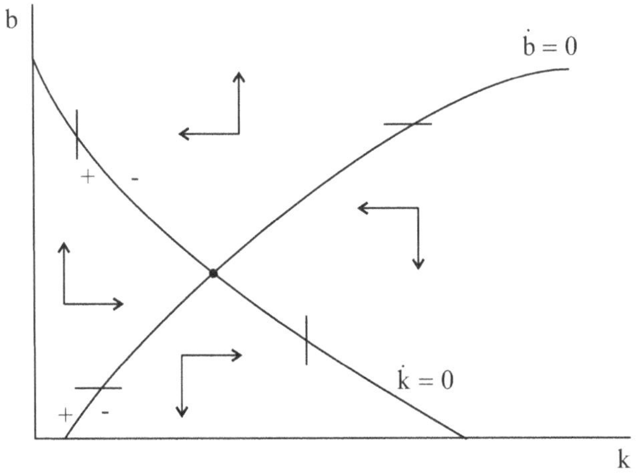

Figure 5.14
Optimal Deficit Ratio
(Infinite Horizon)

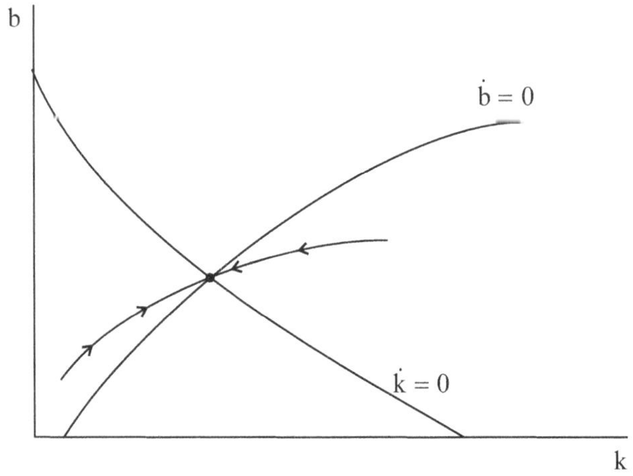

Figure 5.15
Saddle Path

5.3.3 Some Shocks

In the current section, we shall keep track of the adjustment processes released by three distinct shocks:

1) an increase in the saving ratio
2) an increase in the natural rate of labour growth
3) an increase in the discount rate

1) Increase in the saving ratio. At the start, the economy rests in the long-run equilibrium. The deficit ratio and public debt per head do not move. Investment per head and capital per head are uniform. Output and consumption per head do not change. Then, all of a sudden, the saving ratio goes up. As an instantaneous response, the government enhances the deficit ratio so as to stabilize investment per head. By virtue of the budget constraint, the government is in a position to reduce the tax rate so that consumption per head remains unaffected. In the phase diagram, both demarcation lines shift upwards, cf. figure 5.16. Strictly speaking, the economy jumps from the old steady state into the new one.

In the medium run, because of the increase in the deficit ratio, public debt per head piles up. On the other hand, the shock and policy dynamics has no influence on capital per head and output per head, since investment per head did not stir. In addition, the piling up of public debt per head enlarges public interest per head. Therefore, on account of the budget constraint, the government has to lift the tax rate. As time proceeds, the economy approaches a new long-run equilibrium. The deficit ratio and public debt per head do not move any longer. Investment per head and capital per head are still uniform. More exactly, the post-shock value of public debt per head surpasses its pre-shock value, while capital per head stayed put during transition. As a consequence, the shock has no real effects, neither in the short run nor in the long run. This is reverse Ricardian equivalence, so to speak.

2) Increase in the natural rate of labour growth. Initially the economy reproduces itself in the steady state. Public debt per head and capital per head are invariant. Then, abruptly, labour growth speeds up. As an immediate reaction, the government enhances the deficit ratio, thereby depressing investment per head.

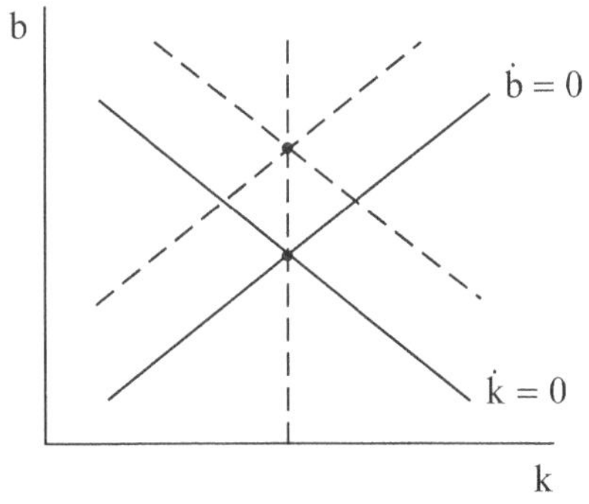

Figure 5.16
Increase in Saving Ratio

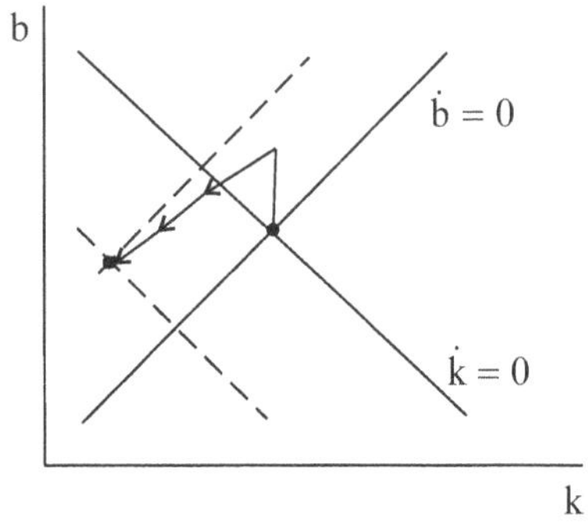

Figure 5.17
Increase in Labour Growth

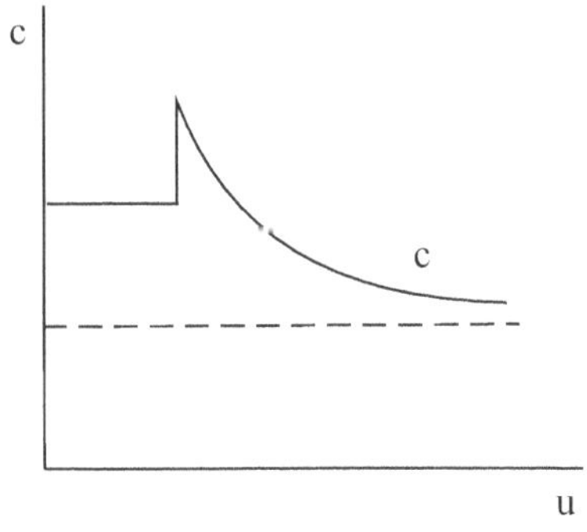

Figure 5.18
Consumption Per Head

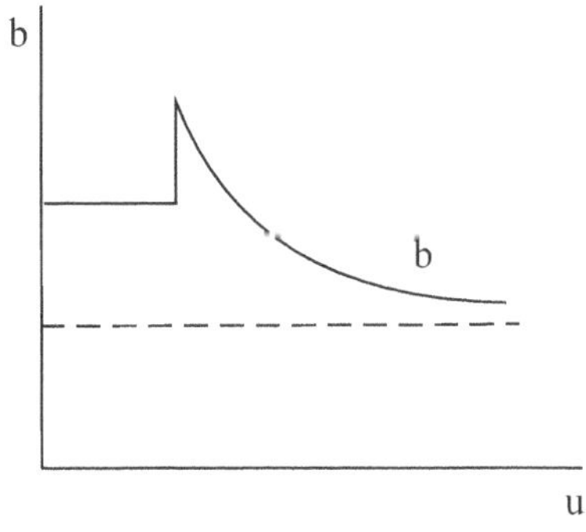

Figure 5.19
Optimal Deficit Ratio

Owing to the budget constraint, the government is able to cut the tax rate, which elevates consumption per head. In the phase diagram, the $\dot{k} = 0$ line is transposed downwards, whereas the $\dot{b} = 0$ line is transposed upwards, cf. figure 5.17. The streamline graphs how the economy develops over time. In the intermediate run, public debt per head is heaped up, while capital per head is run down. Asymptotically the economy converges to a new steady state. Public debt per head and capital per head return to a position of rest. Figures 5.18 and 5.19 plot the associated time paths.

3) Increase in the discount rate. At the start the economy is in the permanent equilibrium. Public debt per head and capital per head are constant. Then arbitrarily future consumption becomes discounted to a higher degree. At once, to counteract this, the government enhances the deficit ratio, thus deteriorating investment per head. As opposed to that, the concomitant tax cut improves consumption per head. In the phase diagram, the $\dot{b} = 0$ line wanders upwards, cf. figure 5.20. In the intermediate term, public debt per head grows, while capital per head declines. In due course the economy gravitates to a new permanent equilibrium. Public debt per head and capital per head settle down. Figure 5.21 depicts the trajectory of the optimal deficit ratio.

5.3.4 Summary

The long-run equilibrium is a saddle point that proves to be stable. Consider for instance a rise in the saving ratio. Without delay the government increases the deficit ratio, hence the disturbance leaves no impact on capital per head. In broader terms, no real effects occur, neither in the short run nor in the long run. As an implication, a fixed saving ratio always can be sustained.

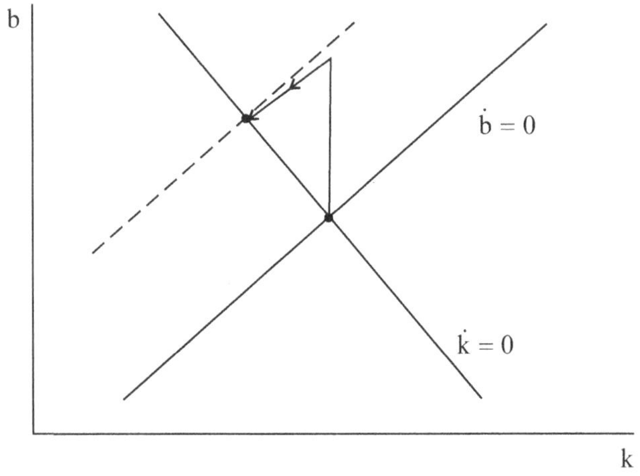

Figure 5.20
Increase in Discount Rate

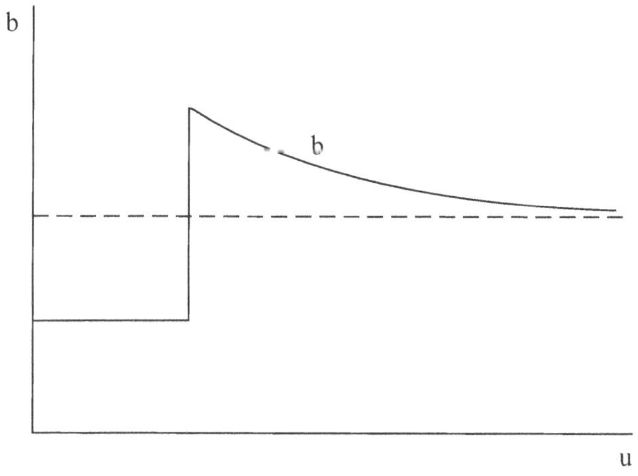

Figure 5.21
Optimal Deficit Ratio

Part II

The Small Open Economy

6 The Solow Model

6.1 Fixing the Deficit Per Head

6.1.1 The Short-Run Equilibrium

The research will be carried out within the following framework. Firms manufacture a homogeneous commodity by employing capital and labour. Let the production function be of the Cobb-Douglas variety $Y = K^{\alpha}N^{\beta}$. Output can be devoted to consumption, investment, government purchases and net exports $Y = C + I + G + H$. Let labour grow at the natural rate $\dot{N} = nN$ with $n = \text{const}$. For the small open economy, the foreign interest rate is given $r^* = \text{const}$. Under perfect capital mobility, the domestic interest rate coincides with the foreign interest rate $r = r^*$. Firms maximize profits under perfect competition, so the marginal product of capital corresponds to the interest rate $\alpha Y/K = r$. This in turn yields the stock of capital. By way of contrast, the wage rate harmonizes with the marginal product of labour $w = \beta Y/N$.

Now have a look at capital dynamics. $Y = K^{\alpha}N^{\beta}$, $\alpha Y/K = r$ and $\dot{N} = nN$ can be reformulated in terms of growth rates as $\hat{Y} = \alpha\hat{K} + \beta\hat{N}$, $\hat{K} = \hat{Y}$ and $\hat{N} = n$, where the hat symbolizes the growth rate. From this one can infer $\hat{K} = \hat{Y} = n$. That is to say, capital, labour and output expand at the natural rate even in the short run. Of course they do so in the long run. This will be stated as $\dot{K} = nK$.

Next catch a glimpse of public debt dynamics. The government provides a certain volume of goods and services per head $G = gN$ with $g = \text{const}$. In addition, the government borrows a fixed amount per head $B = bN$ with $b = \text{const}$. The budget deficit in turn augments public debt $\dot{D} = B$. Moreover the government collects a lumpsum tax $T = tN$ with $t = \text{const}$. The government budget identity is again $B + T = G + rD$. Taking account of the funtional relationships, this can be put as $bN + tN = gN + rD$. Here the government presets purchases per head and the budget deficit per head, while it must adjust the lumpsum tax.

Beyond this we throw some light on the dynamics of foreign assets. Domestic residents earn the interest rate r on foreign assets F, hence the interest inflow totals rF. Disposable income embraces factor income, public interest and the interest inflow, net after tax respectively $Y_d = Y + rD + rF - T$. Households save a constant fraction of disposable income $S = sY_d$. The current account surplus is identical to the excess of savings over the budget deficit and investment E = S − B − I. The current account surplus in turn adds to foreign assets $\dot{F} = E$. Backward substitution affords $\dot{F} = s(Y + rD + rF - T) - B - I$. Paying heed to B + T = G + rD, B = bN, G = gN, $\dot{D}$ = B and nK = $\dot{K}$ = I, this can be written as $\dot{F} = s(Y + rF + bN - gN) - \dot{D} - nK$.

After these introductory remarks, the short-run equilibrium can be described by a system of five equations:

$$Y = K^{\alpha} N^{\beta} \tag{1}$$

$$r = \alpha Y / K \tag{2}$$

$$\dot{D} + \dot{F} = s(Y + rF + bN - gN) - nK \tag{3}$$

$$\dot{D} = bN \tag{4}$$

$$\dot{N} = nN \tag{5}$$

Here α, β, b, g, n, r, s, D, F and N are exogenous, whereas $\dot{D}, \dot{F}, K, \dot{N}$ and Y are endogenous.

Last but not least, it is required to do the analysis in per capita terms. Take the time derivative of foreign assets per head f = F/N to realize $\dot{f} = \dot{F} / N - (F / N)(\dot{N} / N)$. Along these lines, the short-run equilibrium can be represented as follows:

$$y = k^{\alpha} \tag{6}$$

$$r = \alpha y / k \tag{7}$$

$$\dot{d} + \dot{f} = s(y + rf + b - g) - nd - nf - nk \tag{8}$$

$$\dot{d} = b - nd \tag{9}$$

In this version $\dot{d}, \dot{f}$, k and y adapt themselves.

6.1.2 The Long-Run Equilibrium

In the steady state, public debt per head and foreign assets per head come to a standstill $\dot{d} = \dot{f} = 0$. Correspondingly the long-run equilibrium can be characterized by a system of four equations:

$$y = k^{\alpha} \tag{1}$$

$$r = \alpha y / k \tag{2}$$

$$nd + nf = s(y + rf + b - g) - nk \tag{3}$$

$$nd = b \tag{4}$$

In this condition d, f, k and y are endogenous.

Now we shall inquire into the properties of the steady state. Equations (1) and (2) furnish:

$$k = (\alpha / r)^{1/\beta} \tag{5}$$

$$y = (\alpha / r)^{\alpha/\beta} \tag{6}$$

Obviously capital per head and output per head are determined by the foreign interest rate, irrespective of the budget deficit per head etc. Equation (4) can be stated as:

$$d = b/n \tag{7}$$

Then eliminate d in (3) by means of (4) and solve for f:

$$f = \frac{s(y + b - g) - b - nk}{n - rs} \tag{8}$$

From the empirical point of view, it is safe to posit $rs < n$. Accordingly, an increase in the budget deficit per head reduces foreign assets per head.

What is more, the evaluation of (8) leads to a critical level of the budget deficit per head:

$$b' = \frac{s(y-g)-nk}{1-s} \tag{9}$$

If $b \lesseqgtr b'$, then $f \gtreqless 0$. Put differently, under a low deficit per head, the country in question will be a creditor. Under a high deficit per head, however, the country will be a debtor. In addition, the assessment of (9) gives rise to a critical saving ratio:

$$s' = \frac{nk}{y-g} \tag{10}$$

If $s \lesseqgtr s'$, then $b' \lesseqgtr 0$. Properly speaking, as long as the saving ratio is small, there exists a critical surplus per head. But as soon as the saving ratio is large, there exists a critical deficit per head.

As a consequence, for every budget deficit per head there will be a long-run equilibrium. To a certain extent, this deviates from the conclusions drawn for a closed economy, where the budget deficit per head must stay below a critical level. Yet in judging this, one has to keep in mind that the economy cannot be treated as small any longer if the budget deficit per head becomes very large.

Finally a few words will be said on the optimal deficit per head. More accurately, which budget deficit per head maximizes the sum of consumption and government purchases per head $j = c + g$? In answering this question, remember $c = (1-s)(y + rf + b - g)$ as well as (8). The analysis reveals: if $r \lesseqgtr n$, then $dj/db \gtreqless 0$. That means, if the interest rate falls short of the natural rate, the optimal deficit per head becomes very large (i. e. plus infinity). The other way round, if the interest rate exceeds the natural rate, the optimal deficit per head becomes very small (i. e. minus infinity). Beyond that, a very high deficit per head will boost the interest rate, contrary to the assumptions made hitherto.

6.1.3 Stability

The short-run equilibrium can be condensed to a system of two differential equations:

$$\dot{d} = p(d, f) \tag{1}$$

$$\dot{f} = q(d, f) \tag{2}$$

Equation (1) is familiar from section 6.1.1:

$$\dot{d} = b - nd \tag{3}$$

As a byproduct we have $\partial\dot{d} / \partial d = -n < 0$. Then set $\dot{d} = 0$:

$$d = b/n \tag{4}$$

The vertical $\dot{d} = 0$ line can be seen in figure 6.1.

Further substitute (9) into (8) from section 6.1.1, respectively, and rearrange:

$$\dot{f} = s(y + rf + b - g) - b - nf - nk \tag{5}$$

From this one can deduce $\partial\dot{f} / \partial f = rs - n$. Due to $rs < n$, we have $\partial\dot{f} / \partial f < 0$. Besides set $\dot{f} = 0$ and state f explicitly:

$$f = \frac{s(y + b - g) - b - nk}{n - rs} \tag{6}$$

Correspondingly figure 6.1 exhibits the horizontal $\dot{f} = 0$ line. The lesson taught by the phase diagram is that the long-run equilibrium will be stable.

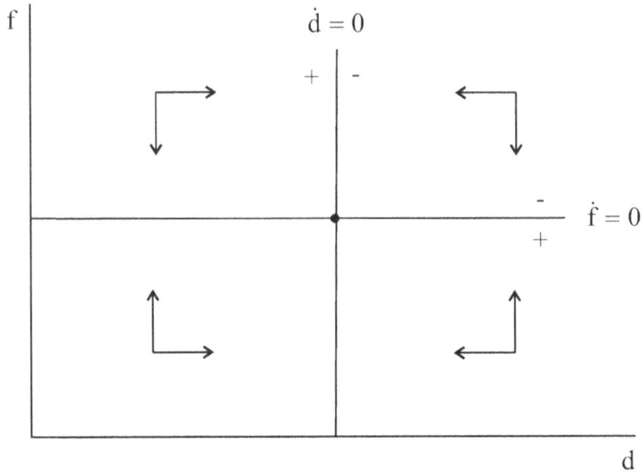

Figure 6.1
Fixed Deficit Per Head
(Solow Model, Open Economy)

6.1.4 Some Shocks

Now we shall discuss the process of adjustment released by four policy measures or shocks in greater details:

1) an increase in the budget deficit per head
2) an increase in government purchases per head
3) an increase in the natural rate of labour growth
4) an increase in the saving ratio.

1) Increase in the budget deficit per head. At the beginning, the economy rests in the long-run equilibrium. The budget deficit and public debt, in per capita terms respectively, do not move. The current account surplus per head and foreign assets per head are uniform. Investment per head and capital per head do not change. Under these circumstances, the government enhances the budget deficit per head. In the phase diagram, the $\dot{d} = 0$ line shifts to the right, while the $\dot{f} = 0$ line shifts downwards, cf. figure 6.2. In the short run, the government action depresses the current account surplus per head. By virtue of the budget constraint, the government is in a position to reduce the tax rate, thereby elevating consumption per head.

In the medium run, owing to the rise in the budget deficit per head, public debt per head accumulates round by round. Similarly, due to the fall in the current account surplus per head, foreign assets per head decumulate period by period. Capital per head does not respond, since investment per head has not been affected. The accumulation of public debt per head causes an expansion of public interest per head. To cover this, the government must lift the tax rate, thus diminishing consumption per head. With the lapse of time, the economy drifts towards a new long-run equilibrium. The budget deficit and public debt, in per capita terms respectively, cease to move. The current account surplus per head and foreign assets per head are again uniform. And investment per head as well as capital per head did not change during transition. Strictly speaking, public debt per head has climbed to a higher level, whereas foreign assets per head have dropped to a lower level. Maybe the country has turned from a creditor into a debtor nation.

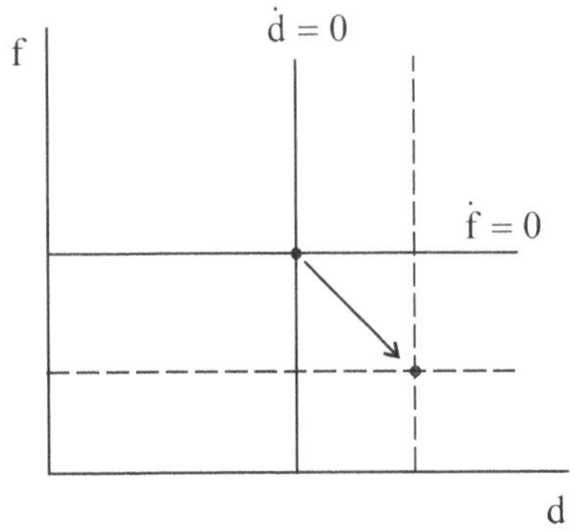

Figure 6.2
Increase in Budget Deficit

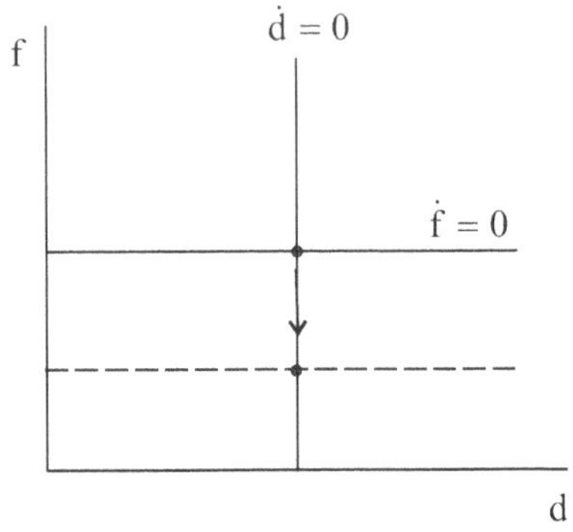

Figure 6.3
Increase in Government Purchases

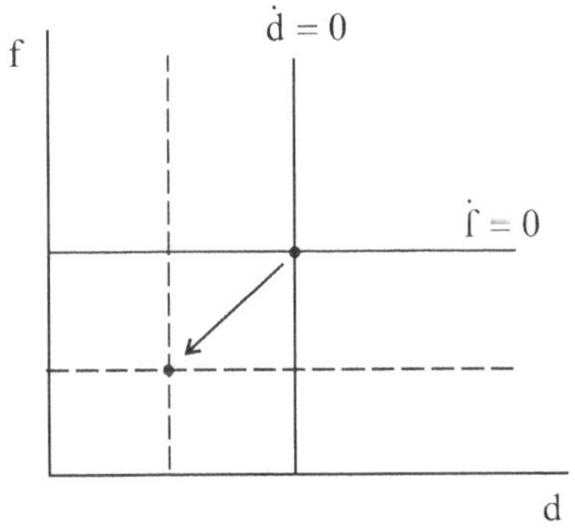

Figure 6.4
Increase in Labour Growth

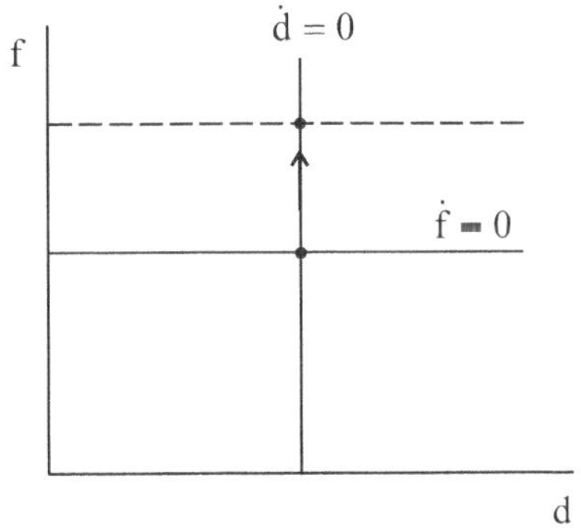

Figure 6.5
Increase in Saving Ratio

2) Increase in government purchases per head. Initially the economy reproduces itself in the steady state. Public debt per head and foreign assets per head are invariant. Then, surprisingly, the government raises its purchases per head. In the phase diagram, the $\dot{f} = 0$ line is transposed downwards, cf. figure 6.3. In the short run, subject to the budget constraint, the government must lift the tax rate. On its part, this lowers savings per head and hence the current account surplus per head. In the medium run, foreign assets per head decline step by step. In the long run, the economy converges to a new steady state. Foreign assets per head have adjusted completely. More exactly, the post-shock value of foreign assets per head is less than their pre-shock value.

3) Increase in the natural rate of labour growth. At the start, the economy is in the stationary equilibrium. Then, abruptly, labour growth accelerates. In the phase diagram, the $\dot{d} = 0$ line glides to the left, while the $\dot{f} = 0$ line glides downwards, cf. figure 6.4. In the intermediate term, public debt per head and foreign assets per head dwindle gradually. And in the long term, they settle down at a deeper level.

4) Increase in the saving ratio. Originally the economy is in the long-run equilibrium. Then, arbitrarily, the saving ratio goes up. In the phase diagram, the $\dot{f} = 0$ line is pushed upwards, cf. figure 6.5. In the short run, the disruption raises the current account surplus per head. In the medium run, therefore, foreign assets per head pile up. Over time, the economy draws close to a new long-run equilibrium. The terminal value of foreign assets per head surpasses their original value. Perhaps the country in question has been converted from a debtor into a creditor nation.

6.1.5 Summary

For every budget deficit per head there exists a long-run equilibrium that proves to be stable. An increase in the budget deficit per head reduces the current account surplus per head, so foreign assets per head come down. And what is more, if the interest rate falls short of the natural rate, a rise in the budget deficit per head improves consumption and government purchases per head. On the other hand, if the interest rate exceeds the natural rate, a rise in the budget deficit per head deteriorates consumption and government purchases per head. Empirical evidence seems to suggest that the government should make loans to the private sector. As a major result, a fixed deficit per head always can be sustained.

6.2 Fixing the Tax Per Head

6.2.1 The Short-Run Equilibrium

The government buys a certain amount of goods and services per head G = gN with g = const. In addition, the government imposes a lumpsum tax T = tN with t = const. The budget deficit can be defined as the discrepancy between public spending and tax proceeds B = G + rD − T. The budget deficit in turn augments public debt $\dot{D} = B$. From this emerges $\dot{D} = gN + rD - tN$.

Now we leave budget dynamics and come to current account dynamics. Disposable income comprehends factor income, public interest and the interest inflow, net after tax respectively $Y_d = Y + rD + rF - T$. Households put aside a given fraction of disposable income for saving purposes $S = sY_d$ with s = const. Savings, diminished by the budget deficit and investment, constitute the current account surplus E = S − B − I. The current account surplus in turn adds to foreign assets $\dot{F} = E$. Backward substitution provides $\dot{F} = s(Y + rD + rF - T) - B - I$. Observe T = tN, $\dot{D} = B$ and $nK = \dot{K} = I$ to acquire $\dot{F} = s(Y + rD + rF - tN) - \dot{D} - nK$.

Along the same lines as in section 6.1.1, the short-run equilibrium can be captured by a system of five equations:

$$Y = K^{\alpha} N^{\beta} \tag{1}$$

$$r = \alpha Y / K \tag{2}$$

$$\dot{D} + \dot{F} = s(Y + rD + rF - tN) - nK \tag{3}$$

$$\dot{D} = gN + rD - tN \tag{4}$$

$$\dot{N} = nN \tag{5}$$

Here α, β, g, n, r, s, t, D, F and N are exogenous, whereas $\dot{D}$, $\dot{F}$, K, $\dot{N}$ and Y are endogenous.

Moreover it is necessary to restate this in per capita terms:

$$y = k^{\alpha} \tag{6}$$

$$r = \alpha y / k \tag{7}$$

$$\dot{d} + \dot{f} = s(y + rd + rf - t) - nd - nf - nk \tag{8}$$

$$\dot{d} = g + rd - t - nd \tag{9}$$

In this version $\dot{d}$, $\dot{f}$, k and y adapt themselves.

6.2.2 The Long-Run Equilibrium

In the steady state, public debt per head and foreign assets per head stop to adjust $\dot{d} = \dot{f} = 0$. Accordingly the long-run equilibrium can be described by a system of four equations:

$$y = k^{\alpha} \tag{1}$$

$$r = \alpha y / k \tag{2}$$

$$nd + nf = s(y + rd + rf - t) - nk \tag{3}$$

$$nd = g + rd - t \tag{4}$$

In this condition d, f, k and y are endogenous.

Next we shall try to find out the steady state values of the endogenous variables. (1) and (2) yield once more:

$$k = (\alpha / r)^{1/\beta} \tag{5}$$

$$y = (\alpha / r)^{\alpha/\beta} \tag{6}$$

Then solve (4) for d:

$$d = \frac{g-t}{n-r} \tag{7}$$

Let be $t < g$. The analysis of (7) yields two distinct cases. As long as the interest rate stays below the natural rate, public debt per head will be positive. In this situation, a long-run equilibrium does exist. But as soon as the interest rate goes beyond the natural rate, public debt per head becomes negative, which appears to be incompatible with $t < g$. Hence one may expect that in this situation a long-run equilibrium does not exist. Finally insert (4) into (3) and reshuffle terms:

$$(n-rs)f = sy - \frac{(1-s)(g-t)r}{n-r} + (1-s)t - g - nk \tag{8}$$

From the empirical point of view it is sound to assume $rs < n$. Thus a cut in the lumpsum tax brings about a diminution in foreign assets per head.

6.2.3 Stability

The short-run equilibrium can be viewed as a system of two differential equations $\dot{d} = p(d, f)$ and $\dot{f} = q(d, f)$.

$$\dot{d} = g + rd - t - nd \tag{1}$$

is well known from section 6.2.1. As a corollary, $\partial\dot{d} / \partial d = r - n$. If $r > n$, then there will be no long-run equilibrium, as has just been established. For the time being, to exclude this, we postulate $r < n$, which entails $\partial\dot{d} / \partial d < 0$. Set $\dot{d} = 0$:

$$d = \frac{g-t}{n-r} \tag{2}$$

Clearly d does not depend on f. For $t < g$ and $r < n$ we have $d > 0$. Figure 6.6 plots the vertical $\dot{d} = 0$ line.

Now get rid of $\dot{d}$ in (8) with the help of (9) from section 6.2.1, respectively:

$$\dot{f} = s(y + rd + rf - t) - g - rd + t - nf - nk \tag{3}$$

In addition verify $\partial\dot{f} / \partial f = rs - n$. Empirically speaking it is valid than $rs < n$, which furnishes $\partial\dot{f} / \partial f < 0$. Then set $\dot{f} = 0$:

$$(n - rs)f = s(y + rd - t) - g - rd + t - nk \tag{4}$$

This involves:

$$\frac{\partial f}{\partial d} = -\frac{(1-s)r}{n - rs} \tag{5}$$

Empirically it holds $rs < n$, so we attain $\partial f / \partial d < 0$. On these grounds, figure 6.6 graphs the downward sloping $\dot{f} = 0$ line. The phase diagram demonstrates that the long-run equilibrium will be stable, cf. figure 6.6.

Coming to an end, we shall give a brief summary. Let be $t < g$. If the interest rate exceeds the natural rate, there will be no long-run equilibrium at all. Conversely, if the interest rate falls short of the natural rate, there will be a long-run equilibrium that proves to be stable. From the empirical point of view, the interest rate is more likely to surpass the natural rate. To a certain extent the open economy contrasts with the closed economy. For the closed economy, as a rule, there will be no long-run equilibrium. As an exception, if the saving ratio is very high, and if the primary deficit per head is extremely low, there will be two long-run equilibria, one of them being stable, the other unstable.

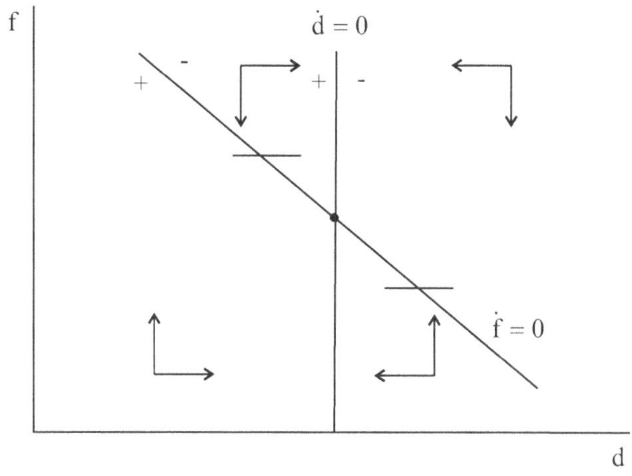

Figure 6.6
Fixed Tax Per Head
(Solow Model, Open Economy)

6.2.4 Some Shocks

1) Tax cut ($r > n$). At the beginning, the economy rests in a long-run equilibrium with $t = g$. The budget is balanced $b = 0$, so there is no public debt $d = 0$. Without loss of generality, let the current account be balanced $e = 0$, too, hence domestic residents do not owe money to foreigners $f = 0$. Investment per head and capital per head are uniform. Under these circumstances, the government reduces the lumpsum tax. In the short run, both the budget and the current account move into deficit, while investment per head does not respond.

In the medium run, owing to the budget deficit, public debt per head accumulates. Likewise, due to the current account deficit, foreign debt per head accumulates. Capital per head, however, remains untouched. As public debt per head grows, the government has to defray more interest per head. This enlarges the budget deficit per head, thereby speeding up the growth of public debt per head. In full analogy, because of the expansion of foreign debt per head, more interest flows out on a per capita basis. The current account deficit per head swells, which accelerates the expansion of foreign debt per head. In the long run, both public debt per head and foreign debt per head proliferate without bounds. The economy enters a vicious circle where the government borrows at home in order to finance the interest payments on public debt. As an immediate consequence, domestic residents borrow abroad in order to finance the interest payments on foreign debt.

Now what difficulties are associated with instability? In the model, there seems to be no hardship. Capital per head is in fact stable, merely public debt per head and foreign debt per head are unstable. The underlying reason is that the budget deficit is covered by raising loans abroad. In the small open economy, the interest rate does not climb as a reaction, thus no crowding out takes place.

But in the real world, as public debt per head and foreign debt per head grow without limits, the economy remains no longer small. On the contrary, the interest rate will be bid up, which decreases capital per head and output per head. As the interest rate tends to explode, capital per head and output per head shrink back to zero. Put another way, there will be fatal crowding out. Ultimately the

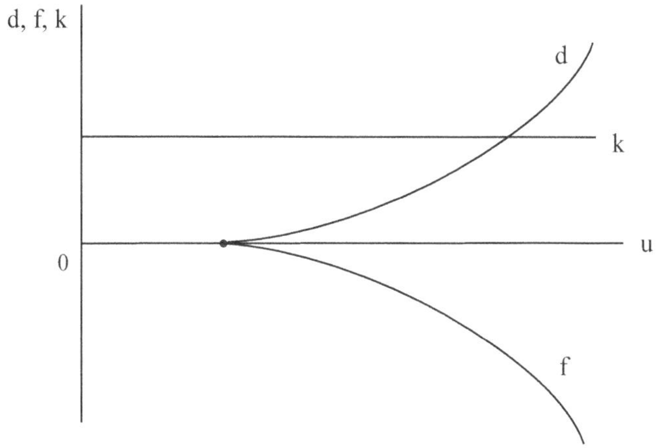

Figure 6.7
Tax Cut (r > n)

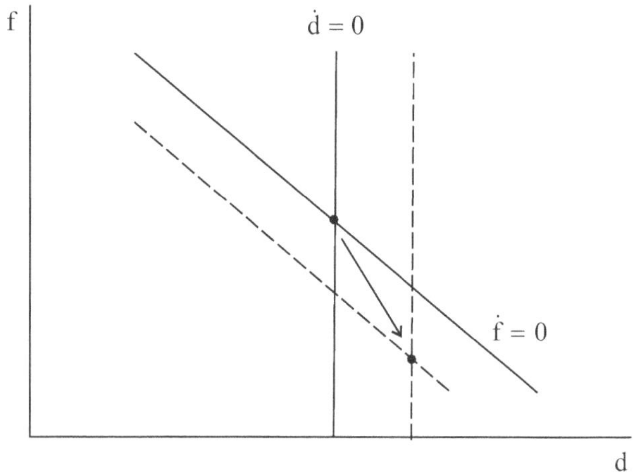

Figure 6.8
Tax Cut (r < n)

economy must break down. For a deeper analysis, see the two-country model in part III. Figure 6.7 illuminates the time paths of the main variables.

2) Tax cut ($r < n$). Initially the economy reproduces itself in the steady state. The budget is balanced, so there is no public debt. Similarly, the current account is balanced, hence there is no foreign debt. Investment per head and capital per head do not change. Then, suddenly, the government curtails the lumpsum tax. In the phase diagram, the $\dot{d} = 0$ locus shifts to the right, while the $\dot{f} = 0$ locus shifts downwards, cf. figure 6.8. In the short run, the policy measure brings both the budget and the current account into deficit. As opposed to that, it leaves no impact on investment per head.

In the medium run, the budget deficit heaps up public debt. Along the same line, the current account deficit builds up foreign debt, in per capita terms respectively. By way of contrast, capital per head stays put. Asymptotically the economy converges to a new steady state. The budget deficit per head and public debt head cease to move. The current account deficit per head and foreign debt per head come to a standstill. Yet investment per head and capital per head are always constant.

6.2.5 Summary

Here two cases can occur. If the interest rate exceeds the natural rate, there will be no long-run equilibrium. Starting from a balanced budget and a balanced current account, a reduction of the lumpsum tax moves both the budget and the current account into deficit. In the long run, therefore, public debt per head and foreign debt per head proliferate without bounds. The other way round, if the interest rate falls short of the natural rate, there will be a long-run equilibrium that turns out to be stable. From the empirical point of view, the interest rate goes beyond the natural rate. In this sense, a fixed tax per head generally cannot be sustained.

7 Overlapping Generations

7.1 Fixing the Deficit Per Head

7.1.1 The Short-Run Equilibrium and the Long-Run Equilibrium

Let us begin with capital dynamics. From $Y = K^{\alpha}N^{\beta}$, $r = \alpha Y/K$ and $N_{+1} = (1+n)N$ one can deduce that $K_{+1} = (1 + n)K$. Now regard the dynamics of public debt. The government spends a given sum per head on goods and services $G = gN$ with $g = \text{const}$. In addition the government borrows a certain amount per head $B = bN$ with $b = \text{const}$. Public debt and the budget deficit this period add up to public debt next period $D_{+1} = D + B$. Moreover the government collects a lumpsum tax $T = tN$ with $t = \text{const}$. The government budget constraint is $B + T = G + rD$. Pay attention to the behavioural functions to arrive at $bN + tN = gN + rD$. Properly speaking, the government presets its purchases per head and the deficit per head, while it accommodates the lumpsum tax.

Third contemplate the dynamics of foreign assets. The savings of the young total $S = \beta\delta Y - \delta tN$, the proof being identical to that presented for the closed economy. The savings of the young in the current period determine public debt, foreign assets and capital in the subsequent period $D_{+1} + F_{+1} + K_{+1} = S$. Combine this with $K_{+1} = (1 + n)K$ and $S = \beta\delta Y - \delta tN$ to reach $D_{+1} + F_{+1} = \beta\delta Y - \delta tN - (1 + n)K$.

Having laid this groundwork, the short-run equilibrium can be characterized by a system of six equations:

$$Y = K^{\alpha}N^{\beta} \tag{1}$$

$$r = \alpha Y / K \tag{2}$$

$$D_{+1} + F_{+1} = \beta\delta Y - \delta tN - (1+n)K \tag{3}$$

$$D_{+1} = D + bN \tag{4}$$

$$bN + tN = gN + rD \tag{5}$$

$$N_{+1} = (1+n)N \tag{6}$$

Here α, β, δ, b, g, n, r, D and N are exogenous, whereas t, D_{+1}, F_{+1}, K, N_{+1} and Y are endogenous.

Further it is required to express this in per capita terms:

$$y = k^{\alpha} \tag{7}$$

$$r = \alpha y / k \tag{8}$$

$$(1+n)d_{+1} + (1+n)f_{+1} = \beta\delta y - \delta t - (1+n)k \tag{9}$$

$$(1+n)d_{+1} = d + b \tag{10}$$

$$b + t = g + rd \tag{11}$$

In this version d_{+1}, f_{+1}, k, t and y adjust themselves appropriately.

In the steady state, public debt per head and foreign assets per head stop to adjust $d_{+1} = d$ and $f_{+1} = f$. Thus the long-run equilibrium can be written as a system of five equations:

$$y = k^{\alpha} \tag{12}$$

$$r = \alpha y / k \tag{13}$$

$$(1+n)d + (1+n)f = \beta\delta y - \delta t - (1+n)k \tag{14}$$

$$nd = b \tag{15}$$

$$b + t = g + rd \tag{16}$$

In this condition d, f, k, t and y are endogenous.

What are the salient features of the steady state? In the same way as in the Solow model one can infer:

$$k = (\alpha / r)^{1/ß} \tag{17}$$

$$y = (\alpha / r)^{\alpha/\beta} \tag{18}$$

$$d = b / n \tag{19}$$

Over and above that, dispense with d and t in (14) by virtue of (15) and (16) to verify:

$$(1+n)f = \beta\delta y - \delta(g + br / n - b) - (1+n)b / n - (1+n)k \tag{20}$$

Evidently, a rise in the budget deficit per head lowers foreign assets per head. To conclude, for every budget deficit per head there exists a long-run equilibrium. This underlines the importance of the results obtained in the Solow model.

7.1.2 Stability and a Shock

The short-run equilibrium can be interpreted as a system of two difference equations:

$$d_{+1} = p(d, f) \tag{1}$$

$$f_{+1} = q(d, f) \tag{2}$$

Equation (1) has been stated explicitly in section 7.1.1:

$$(1+n)d_{+1} = d + b \tag{3}$$

As a byproduct, we have $\partial d_{+1} / \partial d = 1 / (1+n) < 1$. Then equate $d_{+1} = d$ to get:

$$d = b / n \tag{4}$$

Figure 7.1 contains the vertical dd line.

Next explore equation (2). Eliminate d_{+1} and t in equation (9) with the help of equations (10) and (11) from section 7.1.1, respectively:

$$(1+n)f_{+1} = \beta\delta y - \delta(g + rd - b) - d - b - (1+n)k \tag{5}$$

Apparently it is true that $\partial f_{+1}/\partial f = 0$. Then set $f_{+1} = f$:

$$(1+n)f = \beta\delta y - \delta(g + rd - b) - d - b - (1+n)k \tag{6}$$

This implies:

$$\frac{\partial f}{\partial d} = -\frac{1+\delta r}{1+n} < 0 \tag{7}$$

Correspondingly figure 7.1 maps the negatively inclined ff line. Judging by the phase diagram, the long-run equilibrium will be stable.

Besides we examine the dynamic adjustment provoked by an increase in the budget deficit per head. At the start, the economy is in the permanent equilibrium. The budget deficit and public debt, in per capita terms respectively, do not vary. The current account surplus per head and foreign assets per head are uniform. The same applies to investment per head and capital per head. In this situation, the government raises the budget deficit per head. In the phase diagram, the dd line is transposed to the right, whereas the ff line is transposed downwards, cf. figure 7.2.

In the short term, the government action lowers the current account surplus per head, while it has no influence on investment per head. In the intermediate term, public debt per head begins to grow. That is why foreign assets per head begin to decline. And capital per head does not change at all. In due course, the economy approaches a new permanent equilibrium. Public debt per head has mounted to a higher level, whereas foreign assets per head have descended to a deeper level.

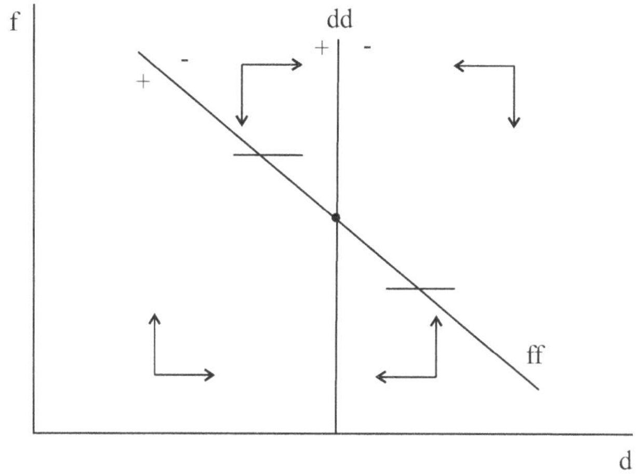

Figure 7.1
Fixed Deficit Per Head
(Overlapping Generations, Open Economy)

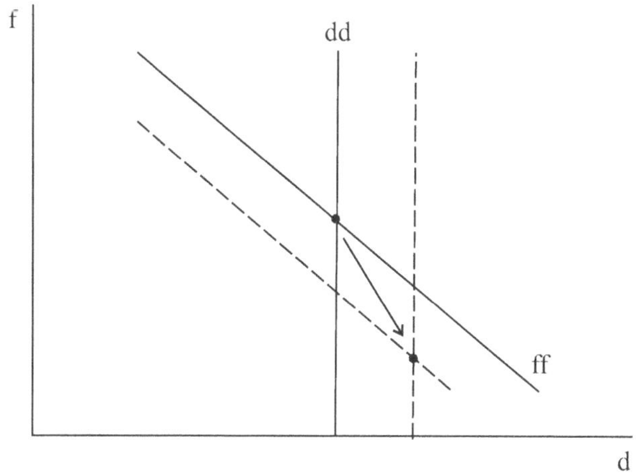

Figure 7.2
Increase in Deficit Per Head

7.1.3 Summary

For every budget deficit per head, there exists a long-run equilibrium that is stable. An increase in the budget deficit per head reduces the current account surplus per head and, hence, foreign assets per head. As an outcome, a fixed deficit per head always can be sustained.

7.2 Fixing the Tax Per Head

7.2.1 The Short-Run Equilibrium and the Long-Run Equilibrium

First of all, catch a glimpse of budget dynamics. The government goes shopping for a specified quantity of goods and services per head $G = gN$ with $g =$ const. In addition the government imposes a lumpsum tax $T = tN$ with $t =$ const. After some manipulations, this yields $D_{+1} = D + gN + rD - tN$. Taking the same avenue as in the preceding sections, the short-run equilibrium can be enshrined in a system of five equations:

$$Y = K^{\alpha}N^{\beta} \tag{1}$$

$$r = \alpha Y / K \tag{2}$$

$$D_{+1} + F_{+1} = \beta\delta Y - \delta tN - (1+n)K \tag{3}$$

$$D_{+1} = D + gN + rD - tN \tag{4}$$

$$N_{+1} = (1+n)N \tag{5}$$

Here α, β, δ, g, n, r, t, D and N are exogenous, whereas D_{+1}, F_{+1}, K, N_{+1} and Y are endogenous.

Now it is convenient to do the research in per capita terms:

$$y = k^{\alpha} \tag{6}$$

$$r = \alpha y / k \tag{7}$$

$$(1+n)d_{+1} + (1+n)f_{+1} = \beta\delta y - \delta t - (1+n)k \tag{8}$$

$$(1+n)d_{+1} = d + g + rd - t \tag{9}$$

In this version d_{+1}, f_{+1}, k and y adapt themselves.

In the steady state, public debt per head and foreign assets per head do no longer move $d_{+1} = d$ and $f_{+1} = f$. Thus the long-run equilibrium can be encapsulated in a system of four equations:

$$y = k^{\alpha} \tag{10}$$

$$r = \alpha y / k \tag{11}$$

$$(1+n)d + (1+n)f = \beta\delta y - \delta t - (1+n)k \tag{12}$$

$$nd = g + rd - t \tag{13}$$

In this condition d, f, k and y are endogenous.

What are the characteristics of the steady state? It still holds:

$$k = (\alpha / r)^{1/\beta} \tag{14}$$

$$y = (\alpha / r)^{\alpha/\beta} \tag{15}$$

Equation (13) furnishes:

$$d = \frac{g-t}{n-r} \tag{16}$$

Let be $t < g$. As long as the interest rate stays below the natural rate, public debt per head will be positive. In this case, a long-run equilibrium does exist. Yet as soon as the interest rate surpasses the natural rate, public debt per head will be negative, which appears to be a contradiction in terms. In this case, no meaningful long-run equilibrium does exist. Essentially this confirms the conclusions drawn in the Solow model. Moreover combine (12) and (13) to establish:

$$(1+n)f = \beta\delta y - \delta t - \frac{(1+n)(g-t)}{n-r} - (1+n)k \tag{17}$$

Let be $r < n$. Then a reduction in the lumpsum tax brings down foreign assets per head.

7.2.2 Stability

The short-run equilibrium can be compressed to a system of two difference equations $d_{+1} = p(d, f)$ and $f_{+1} = q(d, f)$. The first of these equations is familiar from section 7.2.1:

$$(1+n)d_{+1} = d + g + rd - t \tag{1}$$

As a corollary, positing $r < n$, we get $\partial d_{+1}/\partial d = (1 + r)/(1 + n) < 1$. Then equate $d_{+1} = d$ and regroup:

$$d = \frac{g-t}{n-r} \tag{2}$$

Figure 7.3 plots the vertical dd line.

Next put (9) into (8) from section 7.2.1, respectively:

$$(1+n)f_{+1} = \beta\delta y - \delta t - (1+n)k - d - g - rd + t \tag{3}$$

Clearly it is valid that $\partial f_{+1}/\partial f = 0$. In the same vein, equate $f_{+1} = f$:

$$(1+n)f = \beta\delta y - \delta t - (1+n)k - d - g - rd + t \tag{4}$$

From this follows $\partial f / \partial d = -(1 + r)/(1 + n) < 0$. Figure 7.3 graphs the downward sloping ff line. Assembling all component parts, we obtain the phase diagram in figure 7.3. Evidently, the long-run equilibrium turns out to be stable. By the way, the channels of transmission are related to those registered in the Solow model, cf. section 6.2.4.

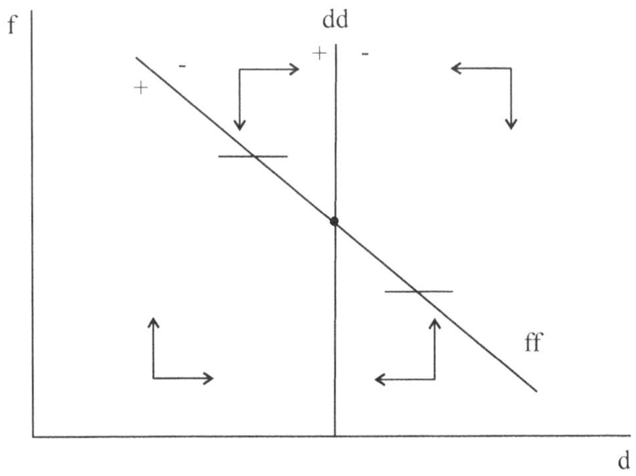

Figure 7.3
Fixed Tax Per Head
(Overlapping Generations, Open Economy)

7.2.3 Summary

Two cases can be distinguished. If the interest rate exceeds the natural rate, there will be no long-run equilibrium. A reduction of the lumpsum tax increases both the budget deficit per head and the current account deficit per head. In the long run, public debt per head and foreign debt per head grow without limits. As opposed to that, if the interest rate falls short of the natural rate, there will be a long-run equilibrium that is stable. Empirically speaking, the interest rate seems to lie well above the natural rate. As an outcome, a fixed tax per head generally cannot be sustained.

Part III

Two Countries

8 The Solow Model

8.1 Fixing the Deficit Per Head

8.1.1 The Short-Run Equilibrium

The analysis will be conducted within the following framework. The two countries i = 1, 2 apply the same technology $Y_i = K_i^\alpha N_i^\beta$. In addition the countries agree in the rate of labour growth $\dot{N}_i = nN_i$. The interest rate coincides with the marginal product of capital $r_i = \alpha Y_i / K_i$. Capital moves freely between countries, thereby equalizing interest rates $r_1 = r_2 = r$.

Now we come to the dynamics of public debt. The government spends a given sum per head on goods and services $G_i = g_i N_i$ with g_i = const. Moreover the government raises a certain amount of loans per capita $B_i = b_i N_i$ with b_i = const. The budget deficit augments public debt $\dot{D}_i = B_i$. Further the government levies a lumpsum tax $T_i = t_i N_i$ with t_i = const. The government budget identity is $B_i + T_i = G_i + rD_i$. Take account of the functional relationships to gain $b_i N_i + t_i N_i = g_i N_i + rD_i$. Here the government presets its purchases per head and the budget deficit per head, while it adjusts the lumpsum tax.

The next point refers to wealth dynamics. Domestic residents earn the interest rate r on foreign assets F_i, so the interest inflow totals rF_i. Disposable income includes factor income, public interest and the interest inflow, net after tax respectively $Y_{di} = Y_i + rD_i + rF_i - T_i$. Households save a specified fraction of disposable income $S_i = sY_{di}$, where the saving ratios are the same size. Wealth is composed of government bonds, foreign bonds and private domestic bonds. Accordingly, savings add to public debt, foreign assets and domestic capital $\dot{D}_i + \dot{F}_i + \dot{K}_i = S_i$. Putting all pieces together, this yields $\dot{D}_i + \dot{F}_i + \dot{K}_i = s(Y_i + rD_i + rF_i - T_i)$. Beyond that, pay attention to $B_i + T_i = G_i + rD_i$, $B_i = b_i N_i$ and $G_i = g_i N_i$ to accomplish $\dot{D}_i + \dot{F}_i + \dot{K}_i = s(Y_i + rF_i + b_i N_i - g_i N_i)$. Besides the foreign assets of country 1 are equivalent to the foreign debt of country 2 $F_1 = -F_2$.

Having laid this foundation, the short-run equilibrium can be captured by a system of six equations:

$$Y_i = K_i^{\alpha} N_i^{\beta} \tag{1}$$

$$r = \alpha Y_i / K_i \tag{2}$$

$$\dot{D}_i + \dot{F}_i + \dot{K}_i = s(Y_i + rF_i + b_i N_i - g_i N_i) \tag{3}$$

$$\dot{D}_i = b_i N_i \tag{4}$$

$$\dot{N}_i = nN_i \tag{5}$$

$$F_1 = -F_2 \tag{6}$$

Here α, β, b_i, g_i, n, s, D_i, F_i, K_i and N_i are exogenous, whereas r, $\dot{D}_i$, $\dot{F}_i$, $\dot{K}_i$, $\dot{N}_i$ and Y_i are endogenous.

Over and above that, is is necessary to do the research in per capita terms:

$$y_i = k_i^{\alpha} \tag{7}$$

$$r = \alpha y_i / k_i \tag{8}$$

$$\dot{d}_i + \dot{f}_i + \dot{k}_i = s(y_i + rf_i + b_i - g_i) - nd_i - nf_i - nk_i \tag{9}$$

$$\dot{d}_i = b_i - nd_i \tag{10}$$

$$f_1 = -f_2 \tag{11}$$

Equation (11) rests on the implicit assumption that both countries have the same population $N_1 = N_2$. In this version r, $\dot{d}_i$, $\dot{f}_i$, $\dot{k}_i$ and y_i adapt themselves.

Then take the sum of equation (9) over both countries, noting $f_1 = -f_2$:

$$\dot{d}_1 + \dot{d}_2 + \dot{k}_1 + \dot{k}_2 = s(y_1 + y_2 + b_1 + b_2 - g_1 - g_2) - n(d_1 + d_2) - n(k_1 + k_2) \tag{12}$$

Incidentally, (7) and (8) provide $k_1 = k_2$ and $y_1 = y_2$. In other words, capital per head and output per head are identical across countries. For the sake of simplicity, we postulate that there is no public sector in country 2 $b_2 = d_2 = g_2 = 0$.

Substitute this together with $k_1 = k_2$ and $y_1 = y_2$ into (12) to arrive at $\dot{d}_1 + 2\dot{k}_1 = s(2y_1 + b_1 - g_1) - nd_1 - 2nk_1$.

As an implication, the short-run equilibrium can be condensed to a system of three equations:

$$y_1 = k_1^{\alpha} \tag{13}$$

$$\dot{d}_1 + 2\dot{k}_1 = s(2y_1 + b_1 - g_1) - nd_1 - 2nk_1 \tag{14}$$

$$\dot{d}_1 = b_1 - nd_1 \tag{15}$$

Here $\dot{d}_1$, $\dot{k}_1$ and y_1 accommodate themselves.

8.1.2 The Long-Run Equilibrium

In the steady state, the motion of public debt per head and of capital per head comes to a halt $\dot{d}_1 = \dot{k}_1 = 0$. Therefore the long-run equilibrium can be described by a system of three equations:

$$y_1 = k_1^{\alpha} \tag{1}$$

$$nd_1 + 2nk_1 = s(2y_1 + b_1 - g_1) \tag{2}$$

$$nd_1 = b_1 \tag{3}$$

In this condition d_1, k_1 and y_1 are endogenous.

Now what we are mainly interested in is how the budget deficit per head impinges on capital per head. Unluckily the system cannot be solved for k_1. As an alternative, b_1 can be stated as an explicit function of k_1. Get rid of d_1 and y_1 in (2) by making use of (3) and (1):

$$b_1 = \frac{2sk_1^{\alpha} - sg_1 - 2nk_1}{1-s} \tag{4}$$

The graphical illustration of equation (4) can be seen in figure 8.1. Obviously there exists a critical level of the budget deficit per head b_1'. As long as the deficit per head stays below the critical value, there will be two long-run equilibria. When the deficit per head matches the critical value, there will be a unique long-run equilibrium. And as soon as the deficit per head surpasses the cricital value, there will be no long-run equilibrium whatsoever. The reason is that the budget deficit of country 1 absorbs world savings entirely. By the way, the critical value can be determined as follows. Differentiate (4) for k_1, set the derivative equal to zero and reshuffle:

$$k_1 = (\alpha s / n)^{1/\beta} \tag{5}$$

Then insert this into (4) to achieve the desired objective.

Finally suppose a state of undercapitalization $s < \alpha$. Imagine that the government of country 1 increases the budget deficit per head. As a consequence, this measure reduces world consumption per head. Consumption per head in country 1 probably falls to a large extent, while consumption per head in country 2 falls to a lesser extent. Under these circumstances, the government action creates "negative externalities".

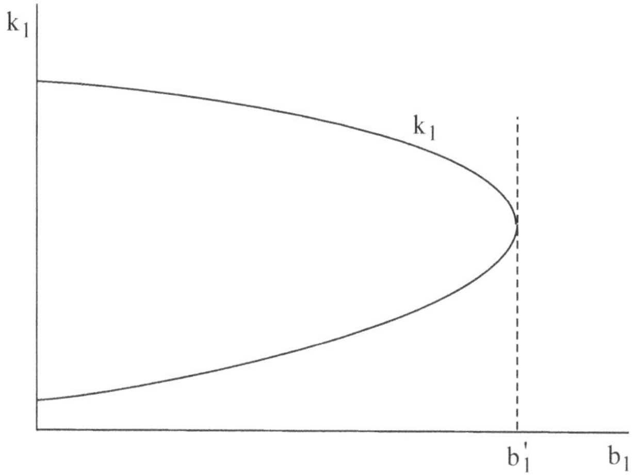

Figure 8.1
Deficit Per Head and Capital Per Head
(Two Countries)

8.1.3 Stability

The short-run equilibrium can be viewed as a system to two differential equations:

$$\dot{d}_1 = p(d_1, k_1) \tag{1}$$

$$\dot{k}_1 = q(d_1, k_1) \tag{2}$$

Equation (1) is well known from section 8.1.1:

$$\dot{d}_1 = b_1 - nd_1 \tag{3}$$

This implies $\partial \dot{d}_1 / \partial d_1 = -n < 0$. Then set $\dot{d}_1 = 0$:

$$d_1 = b_1 / n \tag{4}$$

Figure 8.3 portrays the vertical $\dot{d}_1 = 0$ locus.

In addition dispense with $\dot{d}_1$ and y_1 in (14) by means of (15) and (13) from section 8.1.1, respectively:

$$2\dot{k}_1 = s(2k_1^\alpha + b_1 - g_1) - b_1 - 2nk_1 \tag{5}$$

Figure 8.2 plots how $\dot{k}_1$ varies with k_1. As a finding, there are two steady states k_{11} and k_{12} with $k_{11} < k_{12}$. Here three cases emerge. First, if $k_1 < k_{11}$, then $\dot{k}_1 < 0$. Second, if $k_{11} < k_1 < k_{12}$, then $\dot{k}_1 > 0$. And third, if $k_{12} < k_1$, then $\dot{k}_1 < 0$. That means, the steady state k_{11} will be unstable, but the steady state k_{12} will be stable. Further set $\dot{k}_1 = 0$, which furnishes:

$$2nk_1 = s(2k_1^\alpha + b_1 - g_1) - b_1 \tag{6}$$

This reminds one of the long-run equilibrium, cf. section 8.1.2. Correspondingly equation (6) has two roots. Figure 8.3 displays the horizontal $\dot{k}_i = 0$ loci. Moreover it offers the full phase diagram. As a précis, if the budget deficit per head

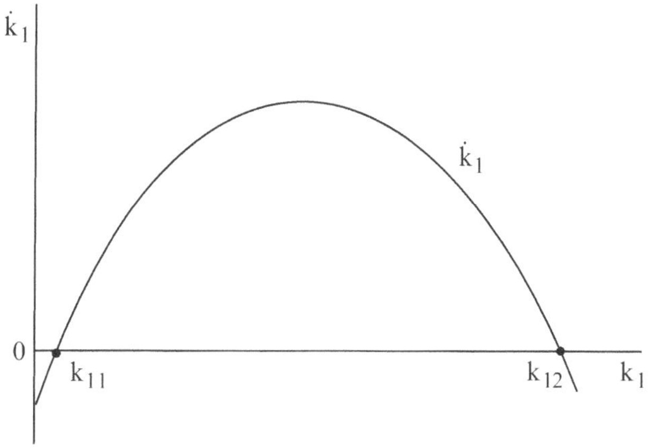

Figure 8.2
Fixed Deficit Per Head
(Two Countries)

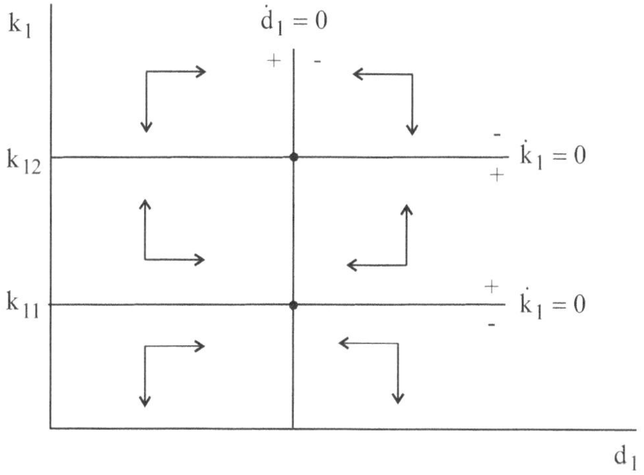

Figure 8.3
Fixed Deficit Per Head
(Two Countries)

falls short of its critical level, there will be two long-run equilibria, one of them being stable, the other unstable. To conclude, a fixed deficit per head generally can be sustained.

8.1.4 An Increase in the Deficit Per Head

Let the budget deficit per head always stay below the critical value $b_1 < b_1'$ and select the stable case. At the beginning, the economy rests in the long-run equilibrium. In country 1 the budget is balanced $b_1 = 0$, so there is no public debt $d_1 = 0$. In both countries the current account is balanced $e_i = 0$, hence neither foreign assets nor foreign debt do occur $f_i = 0$. In both countries, too, investment per head and capital per head are uniform.

Against this background, the government of country 1 lifts the budget deficit per head. In the phase diagram, the $\dot{d}_1 = 0$ line shifts to the right, while the $\dot{k}_1 = 0$ line shifts downwards, cf. figure 8.4. In the short run, the policy measure deteriorates the current account of country 1 and improves the current account of country 2. By way of contrast, the government action depresses investment per head in both countries.

Next have a look at the medium-run effects in country 1. Owing to the budget deficit per head, public debt per head accumulates. Similarly, due to the current account deficit per head, foreign debt per head builds up. And because of the drop in investment per head, capital per head becomes dismantled. What about country 2? By virtue of the current surplus per head, foreign assets per head are heaped up. Likewise, because of the contraction in investment per head, capital per head is run down.

As time goes on, the economy draws near a another long-run equilibrium. In country 1, the budget as well as the current account register a deficit. That is why public debt and foreign debt have been incurred. In both countries, capital per head settles down at a deeper level. In country 2, the current account exhibits a surplus, thus foreign assets have been piled up. As a result, public debt in country 1 crowds out capital both in country 1 and in country 2 to the same degree.

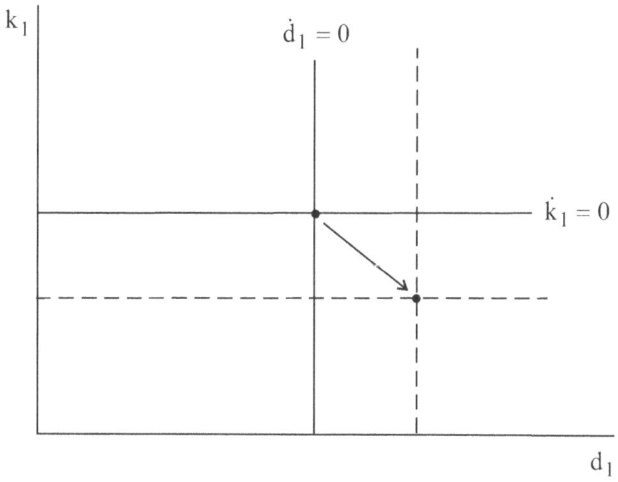

Figure 8.4
Increase in Deficit Per Head
(Two Countries)

8.1.5 The Optimal Deficit Per Head

Now we shall establish the budget deficit per head of country 1 that maximizes consumption per head of country 1. For ease of exposition, we start from the premise that the government of country 1 controls the saving ratio of country 1 (with the help of the budget deficit per head of country 1). Accordingly, we shall try to find out the saving ratio of country 1 that maximizes consumption per head of country 1.

The long-run equilibrium can be characterized by a system of seven equations:

$$y_i = k_i^\alpha \tag{1}$$

$$r = \alpha y_i / k_i \tag{2}$$

$$nf_i + nk_i = s_i(y_i + rf_i) \tag{3}$$

$$f_1 = -f_2 \tag{4}$$

Here f_i, k_i, r and y_i are endogenous.

Next take the sum of (3) over the two countries, observing $f_1 = -f_2$, to achieve $nk_1 + nk_2 = s_1(y_1 + rf_1) + s_2(y_2 + rf_2)$. Paying heed to $k_1 = k_2$ and letting $s_2 = 0$, this simplifies to $2nk_1 = s_1(y_1 + rf_1)$. Therefore the long-run equilibrium can be compressed to a system of four equations:

$$y_1 = k_1^\alpha \tag{5}$$

$$r = \alpha y_1 / k_1 \tag{6}$$

$$nf_1 + nk_1 = s_1(y_1 + rf_1) \tag{7}$$

$$2nk_1 = s_1(y_1 + rf_1) \tag{8}$$

In this version f_1, k_1, r and y_1 adjust themselves.

From (7) and (8) one can deduce $k_1 = f_1$. Moreover insert (5) together with $rf_1 = rk_1 = \alpha k_1^\alpha$ into (8) and rearrange:

$$k_1^\beta = (1+\alpha)s_1 / 2n \tag{9}$$

Once again, which saving ratio of country 1 maximizes consumption per head of country 1? As a first step, consumption per head can be rewritten as $c_1 = (1-s_1)(y_1 + rf_1) = (1-s_1)(1+\alpha)k_1^\alpha$. Further substitute (9) to realize:

$$c_1 = (1-s_1)(1+\alpha)\left[(1+\alpha)s_1 / 2n\right]^{\alpha/\beta} \tag{10}$$

Then differentiate (10) for s_1 and set the derivative equal to zero to reach the optimal saving ratio:

$$s_1^* = \alpha \tag{11}$$

The optimal saving ratio coincides with the capital elasticity, in spite of the fact that households in country 2 do not save at all.

In addition, in which way does consumption per head in country 2 correlate with the saving ratio in country 1? As a baseline take $c_2 = y_2 + rf_2$. Besides eliminate y_2 and f_2 by applying $y_2 = y_1$ and $f_2 = -f_1 = -k_1$ to obtain $c_2 = \beta y_1$. Then take account of (9):

$$c_2 = \beta\left[(1+\alpha)s_1 / 2n\right]^{\alpha/\beta} \tag{12}$$

Put differently, an increase in the saving ratio of country 1 enhances consumption per head in country 2. In a sense, the measure gives rise to positive externalities.

Finally how does this compare with the golden rule? More precisely, what we are searching for is the saving ratio of country 1 that maximizes world consumption per head. The capital intensity to do job is $k_1^\beta = \alpha / n$, as is familiar. Equate this with (9) to check:

$$s_1^{**} = 2\alpha / (1+\alpha) \tag{13}$$

This is the golden-rule saving ratio of country 1. In the numerical example with $\alpha = 0.2$ it holds $s^{**} = 0.33$. Clearly the optimal saving ratio is smaller than the golden-rule saving ratio $s_1^* < s_1^{**}$. As a corollary, under the optimal saving ratio, the interest rate will exceed the natural rate.

Last but not least, a brief comment is in place concerning the simultaneous optimum. The saving ratio of country 1 that maximizes consumption per head of country 1 amounts to $s_1^* = \alpha$, as has just been demonstrated. Beyond that, the saving ratio of country 2 that maximizes consumption per head of country 2 totals $s_2^* = \alpha$, thanks to symmetry. Hence, if both countries optimize simultaneously, the world saving ratio corresponds to the capital elasticity. This in turn is equivalent to the golden rule.

Coming to an end, the optimal saving ratio of country 1 equals the capital elasticity. Over and above that, the optimal saving ratio of country 1 is independent of the saving ratio of country 2.

8.1.6 Summary

Here two cases are to be distinguished. If the budget deficit per head stays below the critical level, there will be two long-run equilibria. On the other hand, if the budget deficit per head surpasses the critical level, there will be no long-run equilibrium at all. Now let the budget deficit per head be sufficiently small and choose the stable case. Further imagine that the government of country 1 increases the budget deficit per head. Then, as a consequence, capital per head declines in both countries. Moreover the foreign position of country 1 worsens, whereas the foreign position of country 2 improves. To sum up, a fixed deficit per head generally can be sustained.

8.2 Fixing the Tax Per Head

8.2.1 The Short-Run Equilibrium and the Long-Run Equilibrium

In full analogy to the preceding sections, the short-run equilibrium can be represented by a system of eleven equations:

$$Y_i = K_i^\alpha N_i^\beta \tag{1}$$

$$r = \alpha Y_i / K_i \tag{2}$$

$$\dot{D}_i + \dot{F}_i + \dot{K}_i = s(Y_i + rD_i + rF_i - t_i N_i) \tag{3}$$

$$\dot{D}_i = g_i N_i + rD_i + rF_i - t_i N_i \tag{4}$$

$$\dot{N}_i = nN_i \tag{5}$$

$$F_1 = -F_2 \tag{6}$$

Here α, β, g_i, n, s, t_i, D_i, F_i, K_i and N_i are exogenous, whereas r, $\dot{D}_i$, $\dot{F}_i$, $\dot{K}_i$, $\dot{N}_i$ and Y_i are endogenous.

Again it is necessary to reformulate this in per capita terms:

$$y_i = k_i^\alpha \tag{7}$$

$$r = \alpha y_i / k_i \tag{8}$$

$$\dot{d}_i + \dot{f}_i + \dot{k}_i = s(y_i + rd_i + rf_i - t_i) - nd_i - nf_i - nk_i \tag{9}$$

$$\dot{d}_i = g_i + rd_i - t_i - nd_i \tag{10}$$

$$f_1 = -f_2 \tag{11}$$

Equation (11) is based on the hypothesis $N_1 = N_2$. In this version r, $\dot{d}_i$, $\dot{f}_i$, $\dot{k}_i$ and y_i adjust themselves.

Take the sum of (9) over the two countries, respecting (11):

$$\dot{d}_1 + \dot{d}_2 + \dot{k}_1 + \dot{k}_2 = s(y_1 + y_2 + rd_1 + rd_2 - t_1 - t_2) - n(d_1 + d_2) - n(k_1 + k_2) \tag{12}$$

In addition, from (7) and (8) one can infer $k_1 = k_2$ as well as $y_1 = y_2$. Moreover we posit the absence of a public sector in country 2 $d_2 = g_2 = t_2 = 0$. In this environment, (12) can be restated as $\dot{d}_1 + 2\dot{k}_1 = s(2y_1 + rd_1 - t_1) - nd_1 - 2nk_1$. Along these lines, the short-run equilibrium can be stripped down to a system of four equations:

$$y_1 = k_1^\alpha \tag{13}$$

$$r = \alpha y_1 / k_1 \tag{14}$$

$$\dot{d}_1 + 2\dot{k}_1 = s(2y_1 + rd_1 - t_1) - nd_1 - 2nk_1 \tag{15}$$

$$\dot{d}_1 = g_1 + rd_1 - t_1 - nd_1 \tag{16}$$

Here $\dot{d}_1$, $\dot{k}_1$, r and y_1 are endogenous.

In the steady state, public debt per head and capital per head stop to adjust $\dot{d}_1 = \dot{k}_1 = 0$. Accordingly the long-run equilibrium can be expressed as follows:

$$y_1 = k_1^\alpha \tag{17}$$

$$r = \alpha y_1 / k_1 \tag{18}$$

$$nd_1 + 2nk_1 = s(2y_1 + rd_1 - t_1) \tag{19}$$

$$nd_1 - g_1 + rd_1 - t_1 \tag{20}$$

In this condition d_1, k_1, r and y_1 have accommodated themselves entirely.

As can easily be seen, the model has the same structure as those derived for a closed economy, cf. section 3.2 (fixed tax rate) and section 3.4 (fixed tax per head) in part I, respectively. For the time being, let the tax per head fall short of government purchases per head $t_1 < g_1$. Under these circumstances there exists a critical tax per head t_1'. If $s < \alpha$ or $t_1 < t_1'$, there will be no long-run equilibrium whatsoever. The other way round, if $s > \alpha$ and $t_1 \geq t_1'$, there will be two long-run equilibria, one of them being stable, the other unstable.

8.2.2 A Tax Cut

Regard the case $s < \alpha$ or $t_1 < t_1^{'}$, thus there will be no steady state. Initially let the economy reproduce itself in a steady state with $t_1 = g_1$. In country 1 the budget is balanced $b_1 = 0$, so there is no public debt $d_1 = 0$. In both countries the current account is balanced $e_i = 0$, hence domestic residents do not owe money to foreigners $f_i = 0$. In both countries, too, investment per head and capital per head do not move. In this situation, the government of country 1 reduces the lumpsum tax. Let us begin with the short-run impact. Owing to the budget constraint, the government of country 1 must increase the budget deficit per head. This measure brings the current account into deficit and curtails investment per head. In country 2 the current account changes into surplus, while investment per head comes down as well.

Next consider the medium-run influence, starting out with country 1. The budget deficit per head contributes to the growth of public debt per head. Similarly the current account deficit per head contributes to the growth of foreign debt per head. And the fall in investment per head leads to the decline of capital per head. As public debt per head accumulates, the government has to disburse more interest per head. On theses grounds the government must further raise the budget deficit per head, thereby speeding up the accumulation of public debt per head. Likewise, as foreign debt per head expands, the interest outflow per head swells. This enhances the current account deficit per head, which in turn accelerates the expansion of foreign debt per head.

At this point we leave country 1 and address country 2. By virtue of the current account surplus per head, foreign assets per head pile up. And due to the drop in investment per head, capital per head becomes depleted. Beyond that, as foreign assets per head build up, more interest per head flows in. This reinforces the current account surplus per head, thus buildung up foreign assets per head more rapidly.

What are the long-run consequences? In country 1, public debt per head and foreign debt per head grow without limits. On its part, this drives capital per head down to zero. In country 2, conversely, foreign assets per head proliferate without bounds. However, capital per head shrinks back to zero in country 2 as well. Ultimately both economies must break down. In other words, the tax cut in country 1 causes fatal externalities.

8.2.3 Summary

As a rule, there will be no long-run equilibrium. Suppose that the government of country 1 reduces the lumpsum tax. In the long run, as an implication, the public debt per head of country 1 tends to explode. This in turn squeezes capital per head down to zero, in country 1 as well as in country 2. As an exception, if the saving ratio is very high and if the primary deficit per head is extremely low, there will be two long-run equilibria, a stable one and an unstable one. To put it into one sentence, a fixed tax per head generally cannot be sustained.

9 Synopsis

To begin with, consider a Solow model of a closed economy where the government fixes the deficit ratio. Under these circumstances, generally, there will be one stable steady state. Now assume that the government instead fixes the tax rate. Then, as a rule, there will be no steady state. As an exception, however, there will be two steady states, one of them being stable, the other unstable. If the government fixes the deficit per head, then generally there will be two steady states, a stable one and unstable one. As an alternative, suppose that the government fixes the tax per head. Then, as a rule, there will be no steady state. But as an exception there will be two steady states, one of them being stable, the other unstable. And what is more, in the overlapping generations model principally the same results can be obtained as in the Solow model.

Next regard an infinite horizon model where the government fixes the deficit ratio. In this situation, there will be one stable steady state. Now imagine that the government instead fixes the tax rate. Then, as a rule, there will be no steady state. Yet as an exception there will be one stable steady state. In place of that, when the government chooses the optimal deficit ratio, there will always be one stable steady state.

At this point we leave the closed economy and turn to the open economy. Contemplate a Solow model where the government fixes the deficit per head. In this enviroment there will be one stable steady state, as opposed to the conclusions drawn for the closed economy. If the government instead fixes the tax per head, then two cases can occur. When the interest rate exceeds the natural rate, there will be no steady state. On the other hand, when the interest rate falls short of the natural rate, there will be one stable steady state. This differs to a certain extent from the findings in the closed economy. In the overlapping generations model, again, basically the same consequences emerge.

Finally address a world economy made up of two countries. At first take a Solow model where the government fixes the deficit per head. Then, generally, there will be two steady states, a stable one and an unstable one. This corresponds to the implications in the closed economy. As an alternative, we postulate that the government fixes the tax per head. Then, as a rule, there will be no steady state. As an exception there will be two steady states, one of them being stable, the other unstable. This confirms the outcome derived in the closed economy.

As a fundamental result, a fixed deficit ratio generally can be sustained. By way of contrast, a fixed tax rate generally cannot be sustained. In full analogy, a fixed deficit per head is feasible in the long run. However, a fixed tax per head is not feasible in the long run. Tables 9.1 to 9.5 present an overview of the conclusions reached.

Table 9.1
Existence and Stability (Ratio Approach)

	fixed deficit ratio	fixed tax rate
closed economy Solow model	1 steady state stable	no steady state
closed economy overlapping generations	1 steady state stable	no steady state
closed economy infinite horizon	1 steady state stable	no steady state

Table 9.2
Existence and Stability (Per-Head Approach)

	fixed deficit per head	fixed tax per head
closed economy Solow model	2 steady states 1 stable	no steady state
closed economy overlapping generations	2 steady states 1 stable	no steady state
open economy Solow model	1 steady state stable	condition
open economy overlapping generations	1 steady state stable	condition
two countries Solow model	2 steady states 1 stable	no steady state

Table 9.3
Sustainability (Ratio Approach)

	fixed deficit ratio	fixed tax rate
closed economy Solow model	sustainable	not sustainable
closed economy overlapping generations	sustainable	not sustainable
closed economy infinite horizon	sustainable	not sustainable

Table 9.4
Sustainability (Per-Head Approach)

	fixed deficit per head	fixed tax per head
closed economy Solow model	sustainable	not sustainable
closed economy overlapping generations	sustainable	not sustainable
open economy Solow model	sustainable	not sustainable
open economy overlapping generations	sustainable	not sustainable
two countries Solow model	sustainable	not sustainable

Table 9.5
Sustainability

fixed deficit ratio	sustainable
fixed tax rate	not sustainable
fixed deficit per head	sustainable
fixed tax per head	not sustainable

10 Conclusion

The present monograph is concerned with the sustainability and optimality of public debt. It consists of three major parts, the closed economy (part I), the small open economy (part II), and two countries (part III). Each part in turn is composed of up to three chapters, the Solow model, the overlapping generations model and the infinite horizon model. Every chapter contains up to four sections. In these sections, the government can fix either the deficit ratio or the tax rate, yet not both at the same time. Analogously, the government can fix either the deficit per head or the tax per head.

First of all have a look at the Solow model of a closed economy (chapter 3). Let us begin with a fixed deficit ratio (section 3.1). An increase in the deficit ratio reduces investment per head and hence capital per head. Properly speaking, the analysis gives rise to a critical deficit ratio. As long as the deficit ratio falls short of the critical level, there will be a long-run equilibrium that proves to be stable. But as soon as the deficit ratio exceeds the critical level, there will be no long-run equilibrium at all. That means, under a low deficit ratio, an increase in the deficit ratio reduces capital per head to a certain extent. Under a high deficit ratio, however, a further increase drives capital per head down to zero.

Moreover there exists an optimal deficit ratio that maximizes the aggregate of consumption and government purchases per head. If the saving ratio is large, the optimal deficit ratio will be positive. In this situation, the government should raise loans in order to restrain capital formation. On the other hand, if the saving ratio is small, the optimal deficit ratio will be negative. In this situation, the government should lend money to the private sector in order to stimulate capital formation. Empirical evidence seems to suggest that the government should extend credit. As a fundamental result, a fixed deficit ratio generally can be sustained.

Next we trace out the process of adjustment induced by an increase in the deficit ratio. First assume that the deficit ratio stays below the critical level. In this case there exists a long-run equilibrium that turns out to be stable. At the start, the economy rests in the long-run equilibrium. The budget deficit and public debt, in per capita terms respectively, do not move. Investment per head and capital per head are uniform. Output and consumption per head do not change. Against this background, the government lifts the deficit ratio. In the short run, output per head remains unaffected. The lift in the deficit ratio curtails investment per head. According to the budget constraint, the government is able to cut the tax rate, thereby raising consumption per head.

In the medium run, owing to the lift in the deficit ratio, public debt per head accumulates round by round. Conversely, due to the fall in investment per head, capital per head decumulates period by period. As capital per head comes down, so do output per head and consumption per head. The accompanying rise in the interest rate, together with the rise in public debt per head, bring up public interest per head. In order to cover this, the government must enhance the tax rate. As time goes on, the economy approaches a new long-run equilibrium. The budget deficit and public debt, in per capita terms, cease to move. Investment per head and capital per head are again uniform. Output and consumption per head do no longer change. More precisely, capital per head settles down at a deeper level.

Second assume that the deficit ratio surpasses the critical level. In this case there exists no long-run equilibrium at all. In the initial steady state, let the deficit ratio stay below the critical level. So public debt per head and capital per head are constant. Then surprisingly the government lifts the deficit ratio well above the critical level. In the short run, this measure crowds out investment per head. In the intermediate run, public debt per head grows step by step. That is why capital per head declines gradually. The decline in capital per head reduces output, income, savings and investment per head, thus accelerating the decline in capital per head. Obviously the economy enters a vicious circle. In the long run, capital per head shrinks back to zero. In other words, crowding out will be fatal. Ultimately the economy must break down.

So far, in section 3.1, we supposed that the government fixes the deficit ratio. Now, in section 3.2, we postulate that the government instead fixes the tax rate. What difference does this alteration make? As a rule there will be no long-run equilibrium whatsoever. Starting from a balanced budget, a reduction in the tax rate increases the deficit ratio and, hence, depresses investment per head. In the long run, as a consequence, public debt per head tends to explode, which squeezes capital per head down to zero. As an exception, if the saving ratio is very high and if the primary deficit ratio is extremely low, there will be two long-run equilibria, one of them being stable, the other unstable.

Besides there exists an optimal tax rate that maximizes the total of consumption and government purchases per head. Here two cases can be distinguished. When the saving ratio is large, the optimal tax rate falls short of the purchase ratio. The other way round, when the saving ratio is small, the optimal tax rate exceeds the purchase ratio. As a principal result, a fixed tax rate generally cannot be sustained. This is in sharp contrast to the conclusions drawn for a fixed deficit ratio: A fixed deficit ratio generally can be sustained indeed. Fortunately the government is free to switch from one regime to the other.

To illustrate this, we keep track of the dynamics generated by a tax cut. In doing this, we posit a normal saving ratio, so there will be no long-run equilibrium. At the beginning, let the economy be in the long-run equilibrium. This requires a balanced budget, thus there is no public debt. Investment per head and capital per head are invariant. Output and consumption per head do not stir. Under these circumstances the government reduces the tax rate. In the short run, this action leaves no impact on output per head. Of course the tax cut improves consumption per head. According to the budget constraint, the government must increase the deficit ratio, thereby deteriorating investment per head.

In the medium run, on account of the increase in the deficit ratio, public debt per head builds up. Similarly, because of the contraction in investment per head, capital per head becomes dismantled. The expansion of public debt per head forces the government to disburse more interest payments per head. To cover this, the government must further elevate the deficit ratio, which speeds up the expansion of public debt per head. Incidentally, as debt income per head climbs, so does consumption per head. In the long run, public debt per head proliferates without bounds. This in turn drives capital per head down to zero. Clearly the economy enters a vicious circle where the government borrows in order to finance the interest payments on public debt. Put another way, there will be fatal crowding out. Eventually the economy must collapse.

As an alternative, consider a fixed deficit per head (section 3.3). The research yields a critical deficit per head. As long as the deficit per head stays below the critical value, there will be two long-run equilibria, a stable one and an unstable one. But as soon as the deficit per head surpasses the critical value, there will be no long-run equilibrium at all. To sum up, a fixed deficit per head generally can be sustained.

In place of that, regard a fixed tax per head (section 3.4). As a rule there will be no long-run equilibrium whatsowever. A diminution of the lumpsum tax raises the deficit per head and, hence, supplants investment per head. In the long run, public debt per head grows without limits. Therefore capital per head shrinks back to zero. As an exception, if the saving ratio is very high and if the primary deficit per head is extremely low, there will be two long-run equilibria, one of them being stable, the other unstable. In this sense, a fixed tax per head generally cannot be sustained. Over and above that, in the overlapping generations model (chapter 4) structurally the same results can be obtained as in the Solow model (chapter 3).

Chapter 5 deals with the infinite horizon model. First assume that the government fixes the deficit ratio (section 5.1). In this environment, the long-run equilibrium is a saddle point that proves to be stable. Suppose that the government increases the deficit ratio. Then, as an instantaneous response, households increase the saving ratio such that capital per head remains intact. The policy measure has no real effects, neither in the short run nor in the long run. That is to say, a fixed deficit ratio generally can be sustained.

What about the process of adjustment released by an increase in the deficit ratio? Initially the economy reproduces itself in the steady state. The budget deficit and public debt, in per capita terms, do not move. Investment per head and capital per head are uniform. Then, all of a sudden, the government lifts the deficit ratio. Without delay, households lift the saving ratio so as to keep investment per head constant. By virtue of the budget constraint, the government is in a position to reduce the tax rate. On balance, consumption per head stays put. In the medium run, the lift of the deficit ratio causes public debt per head to be piled up. As opposed to that, capital per head and output per head do not change, since investment per head is constant. As public debt per head piles up, the government has to pay more interest per head. To cover this, the government must enhance the tax rate. In due course the economy converges to a new steady state. The motion of the budget deficit and of public debt, in per capita terms, comes to a halt. Investment per head and capital per head are still uniform. Strictly speaking, public debt per head reaches a higher level, while capital per head did not change during transition, and the tax rate goes beyond its pre-shock value.

Instead, in section 5.2, we start from the premise that the government fixes the tax rate. Then, as a rule, there will be no long-run equilibrium whatsoever. Yet as an exception, if the discount rate is very low, there will in fact be a long-run equilibrium. Generally a fixed tax rate cannot be sustained.

How does the dynamics of a tax cut look? We posit a normal discount rate, so there will be no long-run equilibrium. At the beginning, let the economy rest in a long-run equilibrium where the tax rate matches the purchases ratio. The budget is balanced, hence there exists no public debt. Investment per head and capital per head do not vary. Then autonomously the government pulls down the tax rate. This induces households to push up the saving ratio at once. In the short run, the tax cut improves consumption per head. Owing to the budget constraint, the government must enlarge the deficit ratio, which worsens investment per head, in spite of the push to the saving ratio. In the intermediate run, public debt per head is heaped up, whereas capital per head is run down. The growth of public debt per head leads to the growth of public interest per head. This compels the government to further enlarge the deficit ratio, thereby accelerating the growth of public debt per head. In the long run, public debt per head tends to explode. This in turn drives capital per head down to zero. Inevitably the economy must disappear from the scene.

As an alternative, in section 5.3, we postulate that the government selects the optimal deficit ratio. The saving ratio, on the other hand, is required to be exogenous. Here the long-run equilibrium is a saddle point that turns out to be stable. Imagine that the saving ratio jumps up on its own. As an instantaneous reaction, to prevent overcapitalization, the government increases the deficit ratio. For that reason, the disturbance has no real influence, neither in the short run nor in the long run. Generally, a fixed saving ratio can be sustained.

Now we discuss the process of adjustment set in motion by a rise in the saving ratio. Originally the economy reproduces itself in the steady state. The budget deficit and public debt, in per capita terms respectively, do not move. Investment per head and capital per head are uniform. Then abruptly households elevate the saving ratio. Without a time lag, the government lifts the deficit ratio such that investment per head remains unaffected. By virtue of the budget constraint, the government is able to cut back the tax rate. Nevertheless consumption per head does not stir. In the medium run, due to the lift of the deficit ratio, public debt per head accumulates. Capital per head and output per head do not answer, as investment per head remains unaffected. Moreover, the rise in public debt per head entails a rise in public interest per head. To cover this, the government must increase the tax rate. With the lapse of time, the economy gravitates towards a new steady state. The motion of the budget deficit and of public debt, on a per capita basis, comes to a standstill. Investment per head and capital per head are always uniform. More exactly, public debt per head attains a higher level, while capital per head stays at the original level.

At this point, we leave the closed economy in part I and turn to the small open economy in part II. In chapter 6, the analysis is conducted within a Solow model. The government fixes either the budget deficit per head or the tax per head. Let us begin with a fixed budget deficit per head (section 6.1). For every budget deficit per head, there exists a long-run equilibrium that is stable. An increase in the budget deficit per head reduces the current account surplus per head and, hence, foreign assets per head. Further it proves useful to distinguish between two cases. As long as the interest rate stays below the natural rate, an increase in the budget deficit per head enhances consumption per head. But as soon as the interest rate surpasses the natural rate, an increase in the budget deficit per head depresses consumption per head. Empirical evidence seems to suggest that the government should make loans to the private sector. Generally a fixed deficit per head can be sustained.

To better understand this, we study the dynamics kicked off by an increase in the budget deficit per head. At the start, the economy is in the permanent equilibrium. The budget deficit and public debt, in per capita terms respectively, do not vary. Likewise the current account surplus and foreign assets, on a per capita basis, do not change. Both investment per head and capital per head are constant. In this condition, the government raises the budget deficit per head. In the short term, this measure lowers the current account surplus per head. By virtue of the budget constraint, the government is in a position to cut the lumpsum tax, thus advancing consumption per head.

In the intermediate term, on account of the rise in the budget deficit per head, public debt per head grows round by round. Conversely, because of the fall in the current account surplus per head, foreign assets decline period by period. By way of contrast, investment per head and capital per head remain untouched. Besides, the expansion of public debt per head is associated with an expansion of public interest per head. To cover this, the government must lift the lumpsum tax, which deteriorates consumption per head. In the long term, the economy draws near another permanent equilibrium. The budget deficit and public debt, in per capita terms, stop to adjust. Similarly, the current account surplus and foreign assets, on a per capita basis, do no longer change. Investment per head and capital per head are still constant. Properly speaking, public debt per head has mounted to a higher level, whereas foreign assets per head have descended to a deeper level. Perhaps the country in question has turned from a creditor into a debtor.

Next consider a fixed tax per head (section 6.2). Two cases emerge from the investigation. If the interest rate exceeds the natural rate, there will be no long-run equilibrium whatsoever. A diminution of the lumpsum tax brings up both the budget deficit per head and the current account deficit per head. In the long run, as an implication, public debt per head and foreign debt per head tend to explode. The other way round, if the interest rate falls short of the natural rate, there will indeed be a long-run equilibrium that is stable. From the empirical point of view, the interest rate appears to go beyond the natural rate. Generally a fixed tax per head cannot be sustained.

To explain this, we keep track of the process precipitated by a tax cut. Let the interest rate be greater than the natural rate, so there will be no long-run equilibrium. Initially let the economy be in a stationary equilibrium where the tax per head corresponds to government purchases per head. The budget is balanced, so there exists no public debt. Without losing generality, let the current account be balanced, too, so there exist neither foreign assets nor foreign debt. Investment per head and capital per head stay put. In this situation, the government curtails the lumpsum tax. In the short run, the budget and the current account move into deficit, while investment per head does not respond.

In the medium run, owing to the budget deficit, public debt builds up, in per capita terms respectively. And due to the current account deficit, foreign debt is heaped up, on a per capita basis. As public debt per head accumulates, the government has to disburse more interest per head. This augments the budget deficit per head, thereby speeding up the accumulation of public debt per head. Along the same lines, as foreign debt per head grows, the interest outflow per head swells. This enlarges the current account deficit per head, thus accelerating the growth of foreign debt per head.

In the long run, both public debt per head and foreign debt per head proliferate without bounds. Apparently the economy enters a vicious circle where the government borrows at home in order to finance the interest payments on public debt. As an immediate consequence, domestic residents borrow abroad in order to finance the interest payments on foreign debt. In the overlapping generations model (chapter 7) essentially the same results can be obtained as in the Solow model (chapter 6).

Finally we address a world economy consisting of two countries (part III). The Solow model serves again as a frame of reference. First regard a fixed deficit per head (section 8.1). The research yields a critical deficit per head. Under a low deficit per head, there will be two long-run equilibria, one of them being stable, the other unstable. However, under a high deficit per head, there will be no long-run equilibrium at all. Let the budget deficit per head be sufficiently small and choose the stable case. Then suppose that the government of country 1 raises the budget deficit per head. This action lowers capital per head, in country 1 as well as in country 2. In addition, it worsens the foreign position of country 1 and improves the foreign position of country 2. Generally a fixed deficit per head can be sustained.

Over and above that, we throw some light on shock dynamics. We posit that the budget deficit per head is less than the critical value and select the stable case. At the beginning, the world rests in the long-run equilibrium. In country 1 the budget is balanced, hence no public debt does exist. In both countries the current account is balanced, so the foreign position amounts to zero. In both countries, too, investment per head and capital per head are uniform. Against this background, the government of country 1 increases the budget deficit per head. In the short run, the current account of country 1 gets into deficit, whereas the current account of country 2 gets into surplus. In both countries investment per head comes down.

What are the medium-run effects? Let us start with country 1. The budget deficit per head leads to the piling up of public debt per head. Analogously, the current account deficit per head causes the piling up of foreign debt per head. And the drop in investment per head calls forth the decumulation of capital per head. Moreover catch a glimpse of country 2. There the current account surplus per head contributes to the accumulation of foreign assets per head. The drop in investment per head provokes the dismantling of capital per head, in country 2 as well.

As time proceeds, the economy approaches a new long-run equilibrium. In country 1 the budget deficit and public debt, in per capita terms respectively, cease to move. The same applies to the current account deficit and to foreign debt, on a per capita basis. Capital per head has settled down at an inferior level. In country 2 the current account surplus per head and foreign assets per head are invariant. There, too, capital per head has adjusted downwards. To put it into one sentence, public debt in country 1 crowds out capital both in country 1 and in country 2.

Second contemplate a fixed tax per head (section 8.2). As a rule, there will be no long-run equilibrium whatsoever. Imagine that the government of country 1 reduces the lumpsum tax. In the long run, therefore, public debt per head grows without limits. That is why capital per head shrinks back to zero, in country 1 as well as in country 2. As an exception, if the saving ratio is very high and if the primary deficit per head is extremely low, there will be two long-run equilibria, a stable on and an unstable one. Generally a fixed tax per head cannot be sustained.

At last we trace out the process originating in a tax cut. Assuming normal saving ratios, there will be no long-run equilibrium. Initially let the economy reproduce itself in a steady state where the tax per head corresponds to government purchases per head. In country 1 the budget is balanced, so there exists no public debt. In both countries the current account is balanced, hence the foreign position equals zero. In both countries, too, investment per head and capital per head are constant. Under these circumstances, the government of country 1 diminishes the lumpsum tax. How is the short-run impact? In country 1, according to the budget constraint, the government must raise the budget deficit per head. This measure brings the current account into deficit and puts a brake on investment per head.

In country 2, on the other hand, the current account changes into surplus, while investment per head slows down.

Beyond that have a look at the medium-run influence. In country 1, owing to the budget deficit per head, public debt per head is heaped up. Similarly, due to the current account deficit per head, foreign debt per head is heaped up. And because of the contraction in investment per head, capital per head becomes depleted. The expansion of public debt per head goes along with an expansion of public interest per head. This enlarges the budget deficit per head, thereby speeding up the expansion of public debt per head. In the same vein, as foreign debt per head grows, more interest per head flows out. This augments the current account deficit per head, thus foreign debt per head grows more rapidly. In country 2, due to the current account surplus per head, foreign assets per head build up. And because of the contraction in investment per head, capital per head becomes depleted, as in country 1. Further, as foreign assets per head accumulate, the interest inflow per head surges. This enhances the current account surplus per head, so foreign assets per head accumulate even faster.

Coming to an end, what are the long-run consequences? In country 1 both public debt per head and foreign debt per head tend to explode. This in turn squeezes capital per head down to zero. In country 2 foreign assets per head become very large, whereas capital per head becomes very small. Ultimately both economies must break down. That means, the tax cut gives rise to fatal externalities.

11 Result

The present monograph is concerned with the sustainability and optimality of public debt. The analysis has been conducted within the framework of neoclassical growth theory. Particularly it proves useful to consider the Solow model, the overlapping generations model and the infinite horizon model. Sustainability refers to the existence and the stability of the long-run equilibrium. Optimality relates to the path of public debt that maximizes discounted utility. The government is in control of three instruments: the government purchase ratio, the budget deficit ratio and the tax rate. For the time being let the purchase ratio be given exogenously. Then the government can follow either of two strategies, it fixes the deficit ratio or the tax rate. If the government fixes the deficit ratio, then according to the government budget constraint the tax rate will be endogenous. On the other hand, if the government fixes the tax rate, the deficit ratio will become endogenous.

First assume a fixed deficit ratio. An increase in the deficit ratio reduces investment per head and hence capital per head. The analysis yields a critical deficit ratio. As long as the deficit ratio falls short of the critical level, there will in fact be a long-run equilibrium that is stable. But as soon as the deficit ratio exceeds the critical level, there will be no long-run equilibrium at all. Under a low deficit ratio, an increase in the deficit ratio reduces capital per head. Under a high deficit ratio, however, a further increase drives capital per head down to zero. Moreover there exists an optimal deficit ratio that maximizes the total of consumption and government purchases per head. When the saving ratio is sufficiently large, the optimal deficit ratio will be positive. In this situation, the government should borrow from the private sector in order to restrain capital formation. Conversely, when the saving ratio is rather small, the optimal deficit ratio will be negative. In this situation, the government should lend to the private sector in order to stimulate capital formation. Empirically speaking, the government should extend credit. As a result, a fixed deficit ratio generally can be sustained.

Second assume a fixed tax rate. As a rule, there will be no long-run equilibrium whatsoever. Starting from a balanced budget, a reduction of the tax rate increases the deficit ratio, thereby crowding out investment per head. In the long run, as a consequence, public debt per head tends to explode, which squeezes capital per head down to zero. As an exception, if the saving ratio is very high and if the primary deficit ratio is extremely low, there will be two long-run equilibria, one of them being stable, the other unstable. In addition there exists an optimal tax rate that maximizes the aggregate of consumption and government purchases per head. When the saving ratio is quite large, the optimal tax rate will stay below the purchase ratio. The other way round, when the saving ratio is comparatively small, the optimal tax rate will surpass the purchase ratio. As an implication, a fixed tax rate generally cannot be sustained. This is in sharp contrast to the conclusions drawn for a fixed deficit ratio. Fortunately the government can switch the regime.

Symbols

A public assets
B budget deficit
C (private) consumption
D public debt
E current account surplus
F foreign assets
G government purchases, public consumption
H net exports
I (private) investment
K (private) capital
N labour
P constant
Q constant
R constant
S (private) savings
T income tax
U discriminant
W welfare
Y output, income
Z budget surplus

a public assets per head
b budget deficit ratio, budget deficit per head
c consumption per head
d public debt per head
e current account surplus per head
f foreign assets per head
g government purchase ratio, government purchases per head
h primary deficit ratio
i investment per head, index 1, 2
j consumption and government purchases per head
k capital per head
n rate of labour growth

p	function
q	function
r	interest rate
s	saving ratio, savings per head
t	tax rate, tax per head
u	time, utility function
v	capital-output ratio
w	wage rate
x	debt-capital ratio
y	output per head, income per head
z	budget surplus ratio
α	parameter of production function
β	parameter of production function
γ	parameter of utility function
δ	parameter of utility function
ρ	discount rate
Π	profits

References

ACEMOGLU, D., Introduction to Modern Economic Growth, Princeton 2009

AGHION, P., HOWITT, P., eds., The Economics of Growth, Cambridge 2009

ALESINA, A., TABELLINI, G., A Positive Theory of Fiscal Deficits and Government Debt, in: Review of Economic Studies 57, 1990, 403 - 414

AMANO, A., International Capital Movements and Economic Growth, in: Kyklos 4, 1965, 693 - 699

ARROW, K. J., BOSKIN, M. J., Eds., The Economcis of Public Debt, New York 1988

ARROW, K. J., KURZ, M., Public Investment, the Rate of Return, and Optimal Fiscal Policy, Baltimore 1970

ASCHAUER, D. A., Finite Horizons, Intertemporal Substitution, and Fiscal Policy, in: Public Finance Quarterly 18, 1990, 77 - 91

ATKINSON, A. B., STIGLITZ, J. E., Lectures on Public Economics, London 1980

AUERBACH, A. J., FELDSTEIN, M., Eds., Handbook of Public Economics, Amsterdam 1987

AUERBACH, A. J., KOTLIKOFF, L. J., Dynamic Fiscal Policy, Cambridge 1987

AZARIADIS, C., Intertemporal Macroeconomics, Oxford 1993

BAILEY, M. J., Note on Ricardian Equivalence, in: Journal of Public Economics 51, 1993, 437 - 446

BARRO, R. J., Are Government Bonds Net Wealth?, in: Journal of Political Economy 82, 1974, 1095 - 1117

BARRO, R. J., The Neoclassical Approach to Fiscal Policy, in: R. J. Barro, Ed., Modern Business Cycle Theory, Cambridge 1989

BARRO, R. J., Reply to Feldstein and Buchanan, in: Journal of Political Economy 84, 1976, 343 - 350

BARRO, R. J., The Ricardian Approach to Budget Deficits, in Journal of Economic Perspectives 3, 1989, 37 - 54

BARRO, R. J., SALA-I-MARTIN, X., Public Finance in Models of Economic Growth, in: Review of Economic Studies 59, 1992, 645 - 661

BARRO, R. J., SALA-I-MARTIN, X., Economic Growth, Cambridge 2004

BARRO, R. J., Macroeconomics, Mason, Ohio 2008

BARTSCH, P., TOLKEMITT, G., Did Growth Theory Deliver any Prescription, Upon Which Public Finance Can Rely?, in: G. Krause-Junk, Ed., Public Finance and Steady Economic Growth, The Hague 1990

BATINA, R. G., IHORI, T., The Chain-Letter Debt Mechanism in a World Economy with Overlapping Generations, Discussion Paper, Toyonaka 1989

BATINA, R. G., IHORI, T., A Dynamic Analysis of the Optimal Provision of a Debt-Financed Public Good in a Small Open Economy, Discussion Paper, Toyonaka 1989

BERNHEIM, B. D., A Neoclassical Perspective on Budget Deficits, in: Journal of Economic Perspectives 3, 1989, 55 - 72

BLANCHARD, O. J., Debt, Deficits, and Finite Horizons, in: Journal of Political Economy 93, 1985, 223 - 247

BLANCHARD, O. J., FISCHER, S., Lectures on Macroeconomics, Cambridge 1989

BLINDER, A. S., SOLOW, R. M., Eds., The Economics of Public Finance, Washington 1974

BOSKIN, M. J., FLEMMING, J. S., GORINI, S., Eds., Private Saving and Public Debt, Oxford 1987

BRÄUNINGER, M., Public Debt and Endogenous Growth, Heidelberg 2003

BRETSCHGER, L., Wachstumstheorie, München 1998

BRUNE, M., Öffentliche Investitionen im langfristigen Wachstumsprozess, Frankfurt 1988

BUCHANAN, J. M., WAGNER, R. E., Democracy in Deficit, New York 1977

BUITER, W. H., Temporary Equilibrium and Long-Run Equilibrium, New York 1979

BUITER, W. H., Time Preference and International Lending and Borrowing in an Overlapping Generations Model, in: Journal of Political Economy 89, 1981, 769 - 797

BUITER, W. H., A Guide to Public Sector Debt and Deficits, in: Economic Policy 1, 1985, 13 - 79

BUITER, W. H., Budgetary Policy, International and Intertemporal Trade in the Global Economy, Amsterdam 1989

BUITER, W. H., Principles of Budgetary and Financial Policy, Cambridge 1990

BUITER, W. H., KLETZER, K. M., Who's Afraid of the Public Debt, in: American Economic Review, Papers and Proceedings 82, 1992, 290 - 294

BUITER, W. H., TOBIN, J., Debt Netrality: A Brief Review of Doctrine and Evidence, in: G. M. von Furstenberg, Ed., Social Security versus Private Saving, Cambridge 1979

BURBIDGE, J. B., Government Debt in an Overlapping Generations Model with Bequests and Gifts, in: American Economic Review 73, 1983, 222 - 227

BURDA, M., WYPLOSZ, C., Macroeconomics, Oxford 2005

BURMEISTER, E., Capital Theory and Dynamics, Cambridge 1980

BURMEISTER, E., DOBELL, R., Mathematical Theories of Economic Growth, New York 1970

BUTKIEWICZ, J. L., On Fiscal Policy and Macroeconomic Stability, in: Public Finance Quarterly 10, 1982, 39 - 47

CARLBERG, M., Is Deficit Spending Feasible in the Long Run?, in: Zeitschrift für Wirtschafts- und Sozialwissenschaften 103, 1983, 409 - 418

CARLBERG, M., Kreditfinanzierung versus Steuerfinanzierung der Staatsausgaben - ein langfristiger Vergleich, in: Kredit und Kapital 17, 1984, 84 - 101

CARLBERG, M., External versus Internal Public Debt - A Theoretical Analysis of the Long-Run Burden, in: Zeitschrift für Nationalökonomie 45, 1985, 141 - 154

CARLBERG, M., Langfristige Grenzen der Staatsverschuldung - Ein Beitrag zur Theorie der optimalen Finanzpolitik, in: Jahrbuch für Sozialwissenschaft 36, 1985, 262 - 273

CARLBERG, M., Public Debt, Taxation and Government Expenditures in a Growing Economy, Berlin 1988

CARLBERG, M., Fiscal Policy, Berlin 1990

CARLBERG, M., Monetary and Fiscal Dynamics, Heidelberg 1992

CARLBERG, M., Open Economy Dynamics, Heidelberg 1993

CARLBERG, M., International Economic Growth, Heidelberg 1997

CARLBERG, M., Intertemporal Macroeconomics: Deficits, Unemployment, and Growth, Heidelberg 1998

CARMICHAEL, J., The Role of Government Financial Policy in Economic Growth, PhD Dissertation, Princeton 1979

CASS, D., On Capital Overaccumulation in the Aggregative, Neoclassical Model of Economic Growth, in: Journal of Economic Theory 4, 1972, 200 - 223

CASS, D., Optimum Growth in an Aggregative Model of Capital Accumulation, in: Review of Economic Studies 32, 1965, 233 - 240

CHIANG, A. C., Fundamental Methods of Mathematical Economics, New York 1984

CHIANG, A. C., Elements of Dynamic Optimization, New York 1992

COHEN, D., How to Evaluate the Solvency of an Indebted Nation, in: Economic Policy 1, 1985, 139 - 156

COHEN, D., DE LEEUW, F., A Note on the Government Budget Restraint, in: Journal of Monetary Economics 6, 1980, 547 - 560

DIAMOND, P. A., National Debt in a Neoclassical Growth Model, in: American Economic Review 55, 1965, 1126 - 1150

DIECKHEUER, G., Makroökonomik, Berlin 2003

DORFMAN, R., An Economic Interpretation of Optimal Control Theory, in: American Economic Review 59, 1969, 817 - 831

DORNBUSCH, R., Dollars, Debts, and Deficits, Cambridge 1986

DORNBUSCH, R., Intergenerational and International Trade, in: Journal of International Economics 18, 1985, 123 - 139

DORNBUSCH, R., DRAGHI, M., Eds., Public Debt Management, Cambridge 1990

DRABICKI, J. Z., TAKAYAMA, A., Money, National Debt, and Economic Growth, in: Journal of Economic Theory 33, 1984, 356 - 367

DUWENDAG, D., Staatsverschuldung - Notwendigkeit und Gefahren, Baden-Baden 1983

EISNER, R., Deficits: Which, How Much, So What?, in: American Economic Review, Papers and Proceedings 82, 1992, 295 - 298

FEHR, H., GOTTFRIED, P., Optimale Verschuldungspolitik und öffentliche Investitionen, in: Finanzarchiv 50, 1993, 324 - 343

FELDERER, B., Ed., Public Pension Economics, Wien 1993

FELDSTEIN, M., Debt and Taxes in the Theory of Public Finance, in: Journal of Public Economics 28, 1985, 233 - 245

FELDSTEIN, M., Perceived Wealth in Bonds and Social Security: A Comment, in: Journal of Political Economy 84, 1976, 331 - 336

FISCHER, S., FRENKEL, J. A., Interest Rate Equalization and Patterns of Production, Trade and Consumption in a Two-Country Growth Model, in: Economic Record 50, 1974, 555 - 580

FLEMMING, J. S., Debt and Taxes in War and Peace: The Case of a Small Open Economy, in: M. J. Boskin et al., Eds., Private Saving and Public Debt, Oxford 1987

FLEMMING, J. S., Debt and Taxes in War and Peace: The Closed Economy Case, in: K. J. Arrow, M. J. Boskin, Eds., The Economics of Public Debt, New York 1988

FOLEY, D. K., SIDRAUSKI, M., Monetary and Fiscal Policy in a Growing Economy, London 1971

FRENKEL, J. A., FISCHER, S., International Capital Movements along Balanced Growth Paths: Comments and Extension, in: Economic Record 48, 1972, 266 - 271

FREY, B. S., Eine einfache Einführung zu Pontryagins Maximum-Prinzip im Wirtschaftswachstum, in: Weltwirtschaftliches Archiv 103, 1969, 213 - 228

FRIED, J., HOWITT, P., Fiscal Deficits, International Trade and Welfare, in: Journal of International Economics 24, 1988, 1 - 22

FRIEDMAN, B. J., Learning from the Reagan Deficits, in: American Economic Review, Papers and Proceedings 82, 1992, 299 - 303

FRIEDMAN, B. M., Day of Reckoning, New York 1988

FRIEDMAN, B. M., HAHN, F. H., Eds., Handbook of Monetary Economics, Amsterdam 1990

VON FURSTENBERG, G. M., Ed., The Government and Capital Formation, Cambridge, Mass. 1980

GALE, D., Money: In Disequilibrium, Cambridge 1983

GALE, D., Pure Exchange Equilibrium of Dynamic Economic Models, in: Journal of Economic Theory 6, 1973, 12 - 36

GANDOLFO, G., Economic Dynamics, Berlin 1996

GANDOLFO, G., International Economics, Berlin 1986

GEBAUER, W., Hg., Öffentliche Finanzen und monetäre Ökonomie, Frankfurt 1985

GIAVAZZI, F., SPAVENTA, L., High Public Debt: the Italian Experience, Cambridge 1988

GORINI, S., Debt, Wealth and the Rate of Growth: An Exercise in Equilibrium Dynamics, in: K. J. Arrow, M. J. Boskin, Eds., The Economics of Public Debt, New York 1988

GORINI, S., The Neoclassical Theory of Public Debt and the Theory of a Long-Run Full-Employment Deficit, in: M. J. Boskin et al., Eds., Private Saving and Public Debt, Oxford 1987

GRILL, R., Der Staat im Modell optimalen Wachstums, Frankfurt 1989

GRÖßL-GSCHWENDTNER, I., Wirkungen staatlicher Budgetdefizite, Tübingen 1990

GROßMANN, H., Auslandsverschuldung, Terms of Trade und überlappende Generationen, Frankfurt 1990

HALIASSOS, M., TOBIN, J., The Macroeconomics of Government Finance, in: B. M. Friedman, F. H. Hahn, Eds., Handbook of Monetary Economics, Amsterdam 1990

HAMADA, K., Economic Growth and Long-Run Capital Movements, in: Yale Economic Essays 6, 1966, 49 - 96

HAMADA, K., Optimal Capital Accumulation by an Economy Facing an International Capital Market, in: Journal of Political Economy 77, 1969, 684 - 697

HAMADA, K., Strategic Aspects of International Fiscal Interdependence, in: Economic Studies Quarterly 37, 1986, 165 - 180

HANSON, J. A., NEHER, P. A., The Neoclassical Theorem Once Again: Closed and Open Economies, in: American Economic Review 57, 1967, 869 - 878

HEILBRONER, R. H., BERNSTEIN, P., The Debt and the Deficit, New York 1989

HELPMAN, E., RAZIN, A., SADKA, E., Eds., Economic Effects of the Government Budget, Cambridge 1988

HERBER, B. P., Ed., Public Finance and Public Debt, Detroit 1986

HOMBURG, S., RICHTER, W. F., Harmonizing Public Debt and Public Pension Schemes in the European Community, in: B. Felderer, Ed., Public Pension Economics, Wien 1993

HONKAPOHJA, S., Ed., The State of Macroeconomics, Oxford 1990

HORI, H., STEIN, J. L., International Growth with Free Trade in Equities and Goods, in: International Economic Review 18, 1977, 83 - 100

HUBER, B., Staatsverschuldung und Allokationseffizienz, Baden-Baden 1990

HUBER, B., Zur Theorie optimaler Staatsverschuldung, in: Finanzarchiv 48, 1990, 434 – 450

IHORI, T., The Golden Rule and the Role of Government in a Life Cycle Growth Model, in: American Economic Review 68, 1978, 389 - 396

IHORI, T., Debt Burden and Intergeneration Equity, in: K. J. Arrow, M. J. Boskin, Eds., The Economics of Public Debt, New York 1988

IHORI, T., Optimal Deficits in a Growing Economy, in: Journal of the Japanese and International Economies 2, 1988, 526 - 542

INTRILIGATOR, M. D., Mathematical Optimization and Economic Theory, Englewood Cliffs 1971

JÄGER, A., KEUSCHNIGG, C., The Burden of Public Debt in Open Economies, in: Finanzarchiv 49, 1992, 181 - 201

JONES, C. I., Introduction to Economic Growth, New York 2002

JUDD, K. L., Debt and Distortionary Taxation in a Simple Perfect Foresight Model, in: Journal of Monetary Economics 20, 1987, 51 - 72

KEHOE, P. J., Coordination of Fiscal Policies in a World Economy, in: Journal of Monetary Economics 19, 1987, 349 - 376

KING, I., FERGUSON, D., Dynamic Inefficieny, Endogenous Growth, and Ponzi Games, in: Journal of Monetary Economics 32, 1993, 79 - 104

KITTERER, W., Sind Steuern und Staatsverschuldung äquivalente Instrumente zur Finanzierung der Staatsausgaben?, in: Kredit und Kapital 19, 1986, 271 - 291

KITTERER, W., Staatsverschuldung und intertemporale Allokation, in: Jahrbücher für Nationalökonomie und Statistik 204, 1988, 346 - 363

KOETZ, A. G., Optimale Staatsverschuldung, Berlin 1983

KOTLIKOFF, L. J., From Deficit Delusion to the Fiscal Balance Rule, in: B. Felderer, Ed., Public Pension Economics, Wien 1993

KRAUSE-JUNK, G., Ed., Public Finance and Steady Economic Growth, The Hague 1990

KRELLE, W., Theorie des wirtschaftlichen Wachstums, Berlin 1988

KURZ, M., The General Instability of a Class of Competitive Growth Processes, in: Review of Economic Studies 35, 1968, 155 - 174

LACHMANN, W., Fiskalpolitik, Berlin 1987

LAITNER, J., Transition Time Paths for Overlapping Generations Models, in: Journal of Economic Dynamics and Control 7, 1984, 111 - 129

LINDBECK, A., WEIBULL, J. W., Intergenerational Aspects of Public Transfers, Borrowing and Debt, in: Scandinavian Journal of Economics 88, 1986, 239 - 267

LIVIATAN, N., Neutrality of Government Bonds Reconsidered, in: Journal of Public Economics 19, 1982, 261 - 270

LORENZ, H. W., Nonlinear Dynamic Economics and Chaotic Motion, Berlin 1993

MASSON, P. R., The Sustainability of Fiscal Deficits, in: IMF Staff Papers 32, 1985, 577 - 605

McCALLUM, B. T., Are Bond-Financed Deficits Inflationary?, in: Journal of Political Economy 92, 1984, 123 - 135

McCANDLESS, G. T., WALLACE, N., Introduction to Dynamic Macroeconomic Theory, Cambridge 1991

MEYER, L. H., The Economic Consequences of Government Deficits, Boston 1983

MICHAELIS, J., Optimale Finanzpolitik im Modell überlappender Generationen, Frankfurt 1989

MICHAELIS, J., Staatsverschuldung als Quelle der Nicht-Neutralität - Ein Beitrag zum Ricardianischen Äquivalenztheorem, in: Kredit und Kapital 22, 1989, 453 - 469

MITCHELL, D. W., The Feasibility of Perpetual Deficits, in: Journal of Macroeconomics 10, 1988, 407 - 419

MODIGLIANI, F., Long-Run Implications of Alternative Fiscal Policies and the Burden of the National Debt, in: Economic Journal 71, 1961, 730 - 755

MODIGLIANI, F., HEMMING, R., The Determinants of National Saving and Wealth, New York 1983

MÜCKL, W. J., Ein Beitrag zur Theorie der Staatsverschuldung, in: Finanzarchiv 39, 1981, 253 - 278

MÜLLER, P., Intertemporale Wirkungen der Staatsverschuldung, Frankfurt 1987

NEHER, P. A., International Capital Movements Along Balanced Growth Paths, in: Economic Record 46, 1970, 393 - 401

NEUMANN, M., Theoretische Volkswirtschaftslehre, München 1991

NOWOTNY, E., Hg., Öffentliche Verschuldung, Stuttgart 1979

O'CONNELL, S. A., ZELDES, S. P., Rational Ponzi Games, in: International Economic Review 29, 1988, 431 - 450

O'DRISCOLL, G. P., Jr., The Ricardian Nonequivalence Theorem, in: Journal of Political Economy 85, 1977, 207 - 210

OKUNO, M., The Burden of Debt and Intergenerational Distribution, in: Keizai Kenkyu 34, 1983, 203 - 215

PEACOCK, A., Is There A Public Debt "Problem" in Developed Countries?, in: B. P. Herber, Ed., Public Finance and Public Debt, Detroit 1986

PERSSON. T., Deficits and Intergenerational Welfare in Open Economies, in: Journal of International Economics 19, 1985, 67 - 84

PHELPS, E. S., The Golden Rule of Accumulation: A Fable for Growthmen, in: Amercian Economic Review 51, 1961, 638 - 643

PHELPS, E. S., Golden Rules of Economic Growth, Amsterdam 1967

PHELPS, E. S., Structural Slumps, Harvard 1994

PHELPS, E. S., SHELL, K., Public Debt, Taxation and Capital Intensiveness, in: Journal of Economic Theory 1, 1969, 330 - 346

RAMSEY, F. P., A Mathematical Theory of Saving, in: Economic Journal 38, 1928, 543 - 559

RAZIN, A., SVENSSON, L.E.O., The Current Account and the Optimal Government Debt, in: Journal of International Money and Fincance 2, 1983, 215 - 224

REITHER, F., Kapitalstock, Staatsverschuldung und rationale Erwartungen, Hamburg 1988

RICARDO, D., On the Principles of Political Economy, and Taxation, London 1817

RICARDO, D., Essay on the Funding Sytem, London 1820

RICHTER, W. F., WIEGARD, W., Zwanzig Jahre "Neue Finanzwissenschaft", in: Zeitschrift für Wirtschafts- und Sozialwissenschaften 113, 1993, 337 - 400

RIEß, A. D., Optimale Auslandsverschuldung bei potentiellen Schuldendienstproblemen, Frankfurt 1988

ROMER, D., Advanced Macroeconomics, New York 2012

ROMMELFANGER, H., Differenzen- und Differentialgleichungen, Zürich 1977

RUFFIN, R. J., Growth and the Long-Run Theory of International Capital Movements, in: American Economic Review 69, 1979, 832 - 842

RUFFIN, R. J., International Factor Movements, in: R. W. Jones, P. B. Kenen, Eds., Handbook of International Economics, Amsterdam 1985

SAINT-PAUL, G., Fiscal Policy in an Endogenous Growth Model, in: Quarterly Journal of Economics 107, 1992, 1243 - 1259

SAMUELSON, P. A., An Exact Consumption-Loan Model of Interest With or Without the Social Contrivance of Money, in: Journal of Political Economy 66, 1958, 467 - 482

SAMUELSON, P. A., Optimum Social Security in a Life-Cycle Growth Model, in: International Economic Review 16, 1975, 539 - 544

SARGENT, T. J., Dynamic Macroeconomic Theory, Cambridge 1987

SARGENT, T. J., WALLACE, N., Some Unpleasant Monetarist Arithmetic, in: Federal Reserve Board of Minneapolis Quarterly Review 5, 1981, 1 - 17

SCARTH, W. M., Can Economic Growth Make Monetarist Arithmetic Pleasant?, in: Southern Economic Journal 53, 1987, 1028 - 1036

SCHIPS, B., Zur Theorie des optimalen Wachstums, Meisenheim 1969

SCHLESINGER, H., WEBER, M., ZIEBARTH, G., Staatsverschuldung - ohne Ende?, Darmstadt 1993

SCHLIEPER, U., Staatsverschuldung im langfristigen Gleichgewicht, in: H. Siebert, Hg., Intertemporale Allokation, Frankfurt 1984

SCHMID, M., Fiscal Ponzi Games in a World Economy, in: F. Gehrels et al., Eds., Real Adjustment Processes under Floating Exchange Rates, Berlin 1990

SCHMID, M., Fiscal Strategies, Foreign Indebtedness and Overlapping Generations, in: Empirica - Austrian Economic Papers 15, 1988, 95 - 115

SEATER, J. J., Ricardian Equivalence, in: Journal of Economic Literature 31, 1993, 142 - 190

SEIDMAN, L. S., The Government Deficit in a Growth Model, in: Journal of Macroeconomics 9, 1987, 593 - 611

SIEBERT, H., Foreign Debt and Capital Accumulation, in: Weltwirtschaftliches Archiv 124, 1988, 618 - 630

SIEBERT, H., Intertemporale Allokation, Frankfurt 1984

SOLOW, R. M., A Contribution to the Theory of Economic Growth, in: Quarterly Journal of Economics 70, 1956, 65 - 94

SOLOW, R. M., Growth Theory and After, in: American Economic Review 78, 1988, 307 - 317

SOLOW, R. M., Perspectives on Growth Theory, in : Journal of Economic Perspectives 8, 1994, 45 - 54.

SOLOW, R. M., Growth Theory: An Exposition, New York 2000

SPAVENTA, L., The Growth of Public Debt: Sustainability, Fiscal Rules, and Monetary Rules, in: IMF Staff Papers 34, 1987, 374 - 399

STEIN, J. L., A Minimal Role of Government in Achieving Optimal Growth, in: Economica 34, 1969, 139 - 150

STEIN, J. L., Monetarism, Amsterdam 1976

STEIN, J. L., Monetarist, Keynesian and New Classical Economics, New York 1982

STIGLITZ, J. E., Methodological Issues and the New Keynesian Economics, in: A. Vercelli, N. Dimitri, Eds., Macroeconomics, Oxford 1992

STIGLITZ, J. E., On the Relevance or Irrelevance of Public Financial Policy, in: K. J., Arrow, M. J. Boskin, Eds., The Economics of Public Debt, New York 1988

TOBIN, J., Asset Accumulation and Economic Activity, Oxford 1980

TOBIN, J., The Monetary-Fiscal Mix: Long-Run Implications, in: American Economic Association, Papers and Proceedings 76, 1986, 213 - 218

TOBIN, J., BUITER, W., Long-Run Effects of Fiscal and Monetary Policy on Aggregate Demand, in: J. L. Stein, Ed., Monetarism, Amsterdam 1976

TOLKEMITT, G., Zur Theorie der langfristigen Wirkungen öffentlicher Verschuldung, Tübingen 1975

TROSTEL, P. A., The Nonequivalence between Deficits and Distortionary Taxation, in: Journal of Monetary Economics 31, 1993, 207 - 227

TURNOVSKY, S. J., SEN, P., Fiscal Policy, Capital Accumulation and Debt in an Open Economy, in: Oxford Economic Papers 43, 1991, 1 - 24

VAN DER PLOEG, R., Handbook of International Macroeconomics, Oxford 1994

VAN MARREWIJK, C., VERBEEK, J., Growth, Budget Deficits, and Fiscal Policies in an Overlapping Generations Model, in: Journal of Economics 53, 1991, 185 - 203

VAUGHN, K. I., WAGNER, R. E., Public Debt Controversies: An Essay in Reconciliation, in: Kyklos 45, 1992, 37 - 49

VOSGERAU, H. J., Optimale Gleichgewichtspfade und optimale Anpassungspfade des wirtschaftlichen Wachstums, in: Jahrbücher für Nationalökonomie und Statistik 179, 1966, 100 - 124

VOSGERAU, H. J., Über optimales wirtschaftliches Wachstum, Basel 1965

WEIL, D. N., Economic Growth, Boston 2009

WEIL, P., Essays on the Valuation of Unbacked Assets, Harvard Ph. D. Thesis 1985

WEIL, P., Permanent Budget Deficits and Inflation, in: Journal of Monetary Economics 20, 1987, 393 - 410

WEIZSÄCKER, R. K., Staatsverschuldung und Demokratie, in: Kyklos 45, 1992, 51 - 67

WELLISCH, D., Intertemporale und internationale Aspekte staatlicher Budgetdefizite, Tübingen 1991

WENZEL, H. D., Öffentliche Kreditaufnahme und öffentliche Investitionen im Wachstumgleichgewicht, in: Kredit und Kapital 19, 1986, 496 - 521

WENZEL, H. D., Staat und Wachstum. Grundlegende Zusammenhänge zwischen staatlicher Aktivität und gesamtwirtschaftlicher Kapitalbildung, in: Volkswirtschaftliche Diskussionsbeiträge, Bamberg 1992

WENZEL, H. D., WREDE, M., Golden Rule Fiscal Policy, in: Schweizerische Zeitschrift für Volkswirtschaft und Statistik 129, 1993, 123 - 149

WILCOX, D. W., The Sustainability of Government Deficits: Implications of the Present-Value Borrowing Constraint, in: Journal of Money, Credit and Banking 21, 1989, 291 - 306

YELLEN, J. L., Symposium on the Budget Deficit, in: Journal of Economic Perspectives 3, 1989, 17 - 21

ZEE, H. H., Government Debt, Capital Accumulation, and the Terms of Trade in a Model of Interdependent Economies, in: Economic Inquiry 25, 1987, 599 - 618

ZEE, H. H., The Sustainability and Optimality of Government Debt, in: IMF Staff Papers 35, 1988, 658 - 685

The manufacturer's authorised representative in the EU is Springer Nature Customer Service Centre GmbH, Europaplatz 3, 69115 Heidelberg, Germany. If you have any concerns regarding our products, please contact ProductSafety@springernature.com

Printed and bound by CPI Group (UK) Ltd, Croydon, CR0 4YY
01/10/2026
02225968-0004